Ella Wheeler Wilcox.

How Salvator Won

AND

OTHER RECITATIONS

BY

ELLA WHEELER WILCOX

Author of "Maurine," "Poems of Passion," "Poems of Pleasure," "Mal Moulée," "Adventures of Miss Volney," "A Double Life," Etc.

New York
EDGAR S. WERNER
1891

PREFACE.

I AM constantly urged by readers and impersonators to furnish them with verses for recitation. In response to this ever-increasing demand I have selected, for this volume, the poems which seem suitable for such a purpose.

In making my collection I have been obliged to use, not those which are among my best efforts in a literary or artistic sense, but those which contain the best dramatic possibilities for professionals. Several of the poems are among my earliest efforts, others were written expressly for this book. In "Meg's Curse," which has never before been in print, and in several others, I ignored all rules of art for the purpose of giving the public reader a better chance to exercise his elocutionary powers.

E. W. W.

CONTENTS.

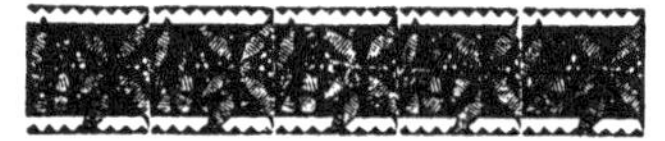

HOW SALVATOR WON.

THE gate was thrown open, I rode out alone,
More proud than a monarch who sits on a throne.
I am but a jockey, yet shout upon shout
Went up from the people who watched me ride out;
And the cheers that rang forth from that warm-hearted crowd,
Were as earnest as those to which monarch e'er bowed.

My heart thrilled with pleasure so keen it was pain
As I patted my Salvator's soft silken mane;
And a sweet shiver shot from his hide to my hand
As we passed by the multitude down to the stand.

The great waves of cheering came billowing back,
As the hoofs of brave Tenny rang swift down the track;
And he stood there beside us, all bone and all muscle,
Our noble opponent, well trained for the tussle
That waited us there on the smooth, shining course.
My Salvator, fair to the lovers of horse,

As a beautiful woman is fair to man's sight—
Pure type of the thoroughbred, clean-limbed and bright,—
Stood taking the plaudits as only his due,
And nothing at all unexpected or new.

And then, there before us the bright flag is spread,
There's a roar from the grand stand, and Tenny's ahead;
At the sound of the voices that shouted "a go!"
He sprang like an arrow shot straight from the bow.
I tighten the reins on Prince Charlie's great son—
He is off like a rocket, the race is begun.
Half-way down the furlong, their heads are together,
Scarce room 'twixt their noses to wedge in a feather;
Past grand stand, and judges, in neck-to-neck strife,
Ah, Salvator, boy! 'tis the race of your life.
I press my knees closer, I coax him, I urge,
I feel him go out with a leap and a surge;
I see him creep on, inch by inch, stride by stride,
While backward, still backward, falls Tenny beside.
We are nearing the turn, the first quarter is past—
'Twixt leader and chaser the daylight is cast.
The distance elongates, still Tenny sweeps on,
As graceful and free-limbed and swift as a fawn;
His awkwardness vanished, his muscles all strained—
A noble opponent, well born and well trained.

I glanced o'er my shoulder, ha ! Tenny, the cost
Of that one second's flagging, will be—the race lost.
One second's weak yielding of courage and strength,
And the daylight between us has doubled its length.

The first mile is covered, the race is mine—no !
For the blue blood of Tenny responds to a blow.
He shoots through the air like a ball from a gun,
And the two lengths between us are shortened to one.
My heart is contracted, my throat feels a lump,
For Tenny's long neck is at Salvator's rump ;
And now with new courage, grown bolder and bolder,
I see him once more running shoulder to shoulder.
With knees, hands and body I press my grand steed ;
I urge him, I coax him, I pray him to heed!
Oh, Salvator! Salvator! list to my calls,
For the blow of my whip will hurt both if it falls.
There's a roar from the crowd like the ocean in storm,
As close to my saddle leaps Tenny's great form,
One more mighty plunge, and with knee, limb and hand,
I lift my horse first by a nose past the stand.
We are under the string now—the great race is done,
And Salvator, Salvator, Salvator won!

Cheer, hoar-headed patriarchs; cheer loud, I say:
'Tis the race of a century witnessed to-day!
Though ye live twice the space that's allotted to
men
Ye never will see such a grand race again.
Let the shouts of the populace roar like the surf
For Salvator, Salvator, king of the turf!
He has broken the record of thirteen long years;
He has won the first place in a vast line of peers.
'Twas a neck-to-neck contest, a grand, honest race,
And even his enemies grant him his place.
Down into the dust let old records be hurled,
And hang out 2.05 in the gaze of the world.

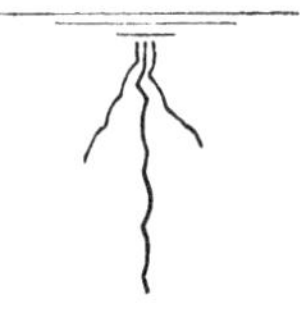

THE GOSSIPS.

A ROSE in my garden, the sweetest and fairest,
Was hanging her head through the long golden hours ;
And early one morning I saw her tears falling,
And heard a low gossiping talk in the bowers.
The yellow Nasturtium, a spinster all faded,
Was telling a Lily what ailed the poor Rose :
"That wild roving Bee who was hanging about her,
Has jilted her squarely, as everyone knows.

"I knew when he came, with his singing and sighing,
His airs and his speeches so fine and so sweet,
Just how it would end ; but no one would believe me,
For all were quite ready to fall at his feet."
"Indeed, you are wrong," said the Lily-belle proudly;
"I cared nothing for him, he called on me once,
And would have come often, no doubt, if I'd asked him,
But, though he was handsome, I thought him a dunce."

" Now, now, that's not true," cried the tall Oleander.
 " He has traveled and seen every flower that grows;
And one who has supped in the garden of princes,
 We all might have known would not wed with the Rose."
" But wasn't she proud when he showed her attention ?
 And she let him caress her," said sly Mignonette;
" And I used to see it and blush for her folly.
 The silly thing thinks he will come to her yet."

" I thought he was splendid," said pretty pert Larkspur,
 "So dark, and so grand with that gay cloak of gold;
But he tried once to kiss me, the impudent fellow!
 And I got offended ; I thought him too bold."
" Oh, fie!" laughed the Almond, "that does for a story.
 Though I hang down my head, yet I see all that goes;
And I saw you reach out trying hard to detain him,
 But he just tapped your cheek and flew by to the Rose.

" He cared nothing for her, he only was flirting
 To while away time, as I very well knew ;
So I turned a cold shoulder on all his advances,
 Because I was certain his heart was untrue."

"The Rose is served right for her folly in trusting
An oily-tongued stranger," quoth proud Columbine.
"I knew what he was, and thought once I would warn her,
But of course the affair was no business of mine."

"Oh, well," cried the Peony, shrugging her shoulders,
"I saw all along that the Bee was a flirt;
But the Rose has been always so praised and so petted,
I thought a good lesson would do her no hurt."
Just then came the sound of a love-song sung sweetly,
I saw my proud Rose lifting up her bowed head;
And the talk of the gossips was hushed in a moment,
And the flowers all listened to hear what was said.

And the dark, handsome Bee, with his cloak o'er his shoulder,
Came swift through the sunlight and kissed the sad Rose,
And whispered: "My darling, I've roved the world over,
And you are the loveliest flower that grows."

PLATONIC.

I KNEW it the first of the summer,
  I knew it the same at the end,
That you and your love were plighted;
  But couldn't you be my friend?
Couldn't we sit in the twilight,
  Couldn't we walk on the shore
With only a pleasant friendship
  To bind us, and nothing more?

There was not a word of folly
  Spoken between us two,
Though we lingered oft in the garden
  Till the roses were wet with dew.
We touched on a thousand subjects—
  The moon and the worlds above,—
And our talk was tinctured with science,
  And everything else, save love.

A wholly Platonic friendship
  You said I had proven to you
Could bind a man and a woman
  The whole long season through,

With never a thought of flirting,
  Though both were in their youth.
What would you have said, my lady,
  If you had known the truth!

What would you have done, I wonder,
  Had I gone on my knees to you
And told you my passionate story,
  There in the dusk and the dew.
My burning, burdensome story,
  Hidden and hushed so long—
My story of hopeless loving—
  Say, would you have thought it wrong?

But I fought with my heart and conquered,
  I hid my wound from sight;
You were going away in the morning,
  And I said a calm good-night.
But now when I sit in the twilight,
  Or when I walk by the sea
That friendship, quite Platonic,
  Comes surging over me.
And a passionate longing fills me
  For the roses, the dusk, the dew;
For the beautiful summer vanished,
  For the moonlight walks—and *you*.

SOLITUDE.

LAUGH, and the world laughs with you ;
Weep, and you weep alone ;
For the sad old earth
Must borrow its mirth,
It has trouble enough of its own.

Sing, and the hills will answer ;
Sigh, it is lost on the air;
The echoes bound
To a joyful sound,
But shrink from voicing care.

Rejoice, and men will seek you ;
Grieve, and they turn and go ;
They want full measure
Of all your pleasure,
But they do not want your woe.

Be glad, and your friends are many ;
Be sad, and you lose them all ;
There are none to decline
Your nectared wine,
But alone you must drink life's gall.

Feast, and your halls are crowded ;
Fast, and the world goes by ;
    Succeed and give,
    And it helps you live,
But it cannot help you die.

There is room in the halls of pleasure
For a long and lordly train ;
    But one by one
    We must all file on
Through the narrow aisles of pain.

GRANDPA'S CHRISTMAS.

IN his great cushioned chair by the fender
An old man sits dreaming to-night,
His withered hands, licked by the tender,
Warm rays of the red anthracite,
Are folded before him, all listless;
His dim eyes are fixed on the blaze,
While over him sweeps the resistless
Flood-tide of old days.

He hears not the mirth in the hallway,
He hears not the sounds of good cheer,
That through the old homestead ring alway
In the glad Christmas-time of the year.
He heeds not the chime of sweet voices
As the last gifts are hung on the tree.
In a long-vanished day he rejoices—
In his lost Used to be.

He has gone back across dead Decembers
To his childhood's fair land of delight;
And his mother's sweet smile he remembers,
As he hangs up his stocking at night.

He remembers the dream-haunted slumber
All broken and restless because
Of the visions that came without number
Of dear Santa Claus.

Again, in his manhood's beginning,
He sees himself thrown on the world,
And into the vortex of sinning
By Pleasure's strong arms he is hurled.
He hears the sweet Christmas bells ringing,
"Repent ye, repent ye, and pray;"
But he joins with his comrades in singing
A bacchanal lay.

Again he stands under the holly
With a blushing face lifted to his;
For love has been stronger than folly,
And has turned him from vice unto bliss;
And the whole world is lit with new glory
As the sweet vows are uttered again,
While the Christmas bells tell the old story
Of peace unto men.

Again, with his little brood 'round him,
He sits by the fair mother-wife;
He knows that the angels have crowned him
With the truest, best riches of life;
And the hearts of the children, untroubled,
Are filled with the gay Christmas-tide;
And the gifts for sweet Maudie are doubled,
'Tis her birthday, beside.

Again,—ah, dear Jesus, have pity—
 He finds in the chill, waning day,
That one has come home from the city—
 Frail Maudie, whom love led astray.
She lies with her babe on her bosom—
 Half-hid by the snow's fleecy spread;
A bud and a poor trampled blossom—
 And both are quite dead.

So fair and so fragile! just twenty—
 How mocking the bells sound to-night!
She starved in this great land of plenty,
 When she tried to grope back to the light.
Christ, are Thy disciples inhuman,
 Or only for *men* hast Thou died?
No mercy is shown to a woman
 Who once steps aside.

Again he leans over the shrouded
 Still form of the mother and wife;
Very lonely the way seems, and clouded,
 As he looks down the vista of life.
With the sweet Christmas chimes there is blended
 The knell for a life that is done,
And he knows that his joys are all ended
 And his waiting begun.

So long have the years been, so lonely,
 As he counts them by Christmases gone.
"I am homesick," he murmurs; "if only
 The Angel would lead the way on.

I am cold, in this chill winter weather;
   Why, Maudie, dear, where have you been?
And you, too, sweet wife—and together—
   O Christ, let me in."

The children ran in from the hallway,
   "Were you calling us, grandpa?" they said.
Then shrank, with that fear that comes alway
   When young eyes look their first on the dead.
The freedom so longed for is given.
   The children speak low and draw near:
"Dear grandpa keeps Christmas in Heaven
   With grandma, this year."

AFTER THE ENGAGEMENT.

WELL, Mabel, 'tis over and ended—
The ball I wrote was to be;
And oh! it was perfectly splendid—
If you *could* have been here to see.
I've a thousand things to write you
That I know you are wanting to hear,
And one, that is sure to delight you—
I am wearing Joe's diamond, my dear!

Yes, mamma is quite ecstatic
That I am engaged to Joe;
She thinks I am rather erratic,
And feared that I might say "no."
But, Mabel, I'm twenty-seven
(Though nobody *dreams* it, dear),
And a fortune like Joe's isn't given
To lay at one's feet each year.

You know my old fancy for Harry—
Or, at least, I am certain you guessed
That it took all my sense not to marry
And go with that fellow out west.

But that was my very first season—
  And Harry was poor as could be,
And mamma's good practical reason
  Took all the romance out of me.

She whisked me off over the ocean,
  And had me presented at court,
And got me all out of the notion
  That ranch life out west was my forte.
Of course I have never repented—
  I'm not such a goose of a thing;
But after I had consented
  To Joe—and he gave me the ring—

I felt such a queer sensation.
  I seemed to go into a trance,
Away from the music's pulsation,
  Away from the lights and the dance.
And the wind o'er the wild prairie
  Seemed blowing strong and free,
And it seemed not Joe, but Harry
  Who was standing there close to me.

And the funniest feverish feeling
  Went up from my fcct to my head,
With little chills after it stealing—
  And my hands got as numb as the dead.
A moment, and then it was over:
  The diamond blazed up in my eyes,
And I saw in the face of my lover
  A questioning, strange surprise.

Maybe 'twas the scent of the flowers,
  That heavy with fragrance bloomed near,
But I didn't feel natural for hours;
  It was odd now, wasn't it, dear?
Write soon to your fortunate Clara
  Who has carried the prize away,
And say you'll come on when I marry;
  I think it will happen in May.

THE WATCHER.

"I THINK I hear the sound of horses' feet
Beating upon the graveled avenue.
Go to the window that looks on the street,
He would not let me die alone, I knew."
Back to the couch the patient watcher passed,
And said: "It is the wailing of the blast."

She turned upon her couch and, seeming, slept,
The long, dark lashes shadowing her cheek;
And on and on the weary moments crept,
When suddenly the watcher heard her speak:
"I think I hear the sound of horses' hoofs—"
And answered, "'Tis the rain upon the roofs."

Unbroken silence, quiet, deep, profound.
The restless sleeper turns: "How dark, how late!
What is it that I hear—a trampling sound?
I think there is a horseman at the gate."
The watcher turns away her eyes tear-blind:
"It is the shutter beating in the wind."

The dread hours passed ; the patient clock ticked
on ;
The weary watcher moved not from her place.
The gray dim shadows of the early dawn
Caught sudden glory from the sleeper's face.
"He comes ! my love ! I knew he would !" she
cried ;
And smiling sweetly in her slumbers, died.

FALSE.

FALSE! Good God, I am dreaming!
No, no, it never can be—
You who are so true in seeming,
You, false to your vows and me?
My wife and my fair boy's mother
The star of my life—my queen—
To yield herself to another
Like some light Magdalene!

Proofs! what are proofs—I defy them!
They never can shake my trust;
If you look in my face and deny them
I will trample them into the dust.
For whenever I read of the glory
Of the realms of Paradise,
I sought for the truth of the story
And found it in your sweet eyes.

Why, you are the shy young creature
I wooed in her maiden grace;
There was purity in each feature,
And my heaven I found in your face.
And, "not only married but mated,"
I would say in my pride and joy;
And our hopes were all consummated
When the angels gave us our boy.

Now you could not blot that beginning
  So beautiful, pure and true,
With a record of wicked sinning
  As a common woman might do.
Look up in your old frank fashion,
  With your smile so free from art;
And say that no guilty passion
  Has ever crept into your heart.

How pallid you are, and you tremble!
  You are hiding your face from view!
"Tho' a sinner, you cannot dissemble"—
  My God! then the tale is true?
True and the sun above us
  Shines on in the summer skies?
And men say the angels love us,
  And that God is good and wise.

Yet he lets a wanton thing like you
  Ruin my home and my name!
Get out of my sight ere I strike you
  Dead in your shameless shame!
No, no, I was wild, I was brutal;
  I would not take your life,
For the efforts of death would be futile
  To wipe out the sin of a wife.
Wife—why, that word has seemed sainted,
  I uttered it like a prayer.
And now to think it is tainted—
  Christ! how much we can bear!

"Slay you!" my boy's stained mother—
  Nay, that would not punish, or save;
A soul that has outraged another
  Finds no sudden peace in the grave.
I will leave you here to *remember*
  The Eden that was your own,
While on toward my life's December
  I walk in the dark alone.

THE PHANTOM BALL.

YOU remember the hall on the corner?
To-night as I walked down street
I heard the sound of music,
And the rhythmic beat and beat,
In time to the pulsing measure
Of lightly tripping feet.

And I turned and entered the doorway—
It was years since I had been there—
Years, and life seemed altered:
Pleasure had changed to care.
But again I was hearing the music
And watching the dancers fair.

And then, as I stood and listened,
The music lost its glee;
And instead of the merry waltzers
There were ghosts of the Used-to-be—
Ghosts of the pleasure-seekers
Who once had danced with me.

Oh, 'twas a ghastly picture!
  Oh, 'twas a gruesome crowd!
Each bearing a skull on his shoulder,
  Each trailing a long white shroud,
As they whirled in the dance together,
  And the music shrieked aloud.

As they danced, their dry bones rattled
  Like shutters in a blast;
And they stared from eyeless sockets
  On me as they circled past;
And the music that kept them whirling
  Was a funeral dirge played fast.

Some of them wore their face-cloths,
  Others were rotted away.
Some had mould on their garments,
  And some seemed dead but a day.
Corpses all, but I knew them
  As friends, once blithe and gay.

Beauty and strength and manhood—
  And this was the end of it all:
Nothing but phantoms whirling
  In a ghastly skeleton ball.
But the music ceased—and they vanished,
  And I came away from the hall.

THE KINGDOM OF LOVE.

IN the dawn of the day when the sea and the earth
Reflected the sunrise above,
I set forth with a heart full of courage and mirth
To seek for the Kingdom of Love.
I asked of a Poet I met on the way
Which cross-road would lead me aright.
And he said: "Follow me, and ere long you shall see
Its glittering turrets of light."

And soon in the distance a city shone fair.
"Look yonder," he said; "how it gleams!"
But alas! for the hopes that were doomed to despair,
It was only the "Kingdom of Dreams."
Then the next man I asked was a gay Cavalier,
And he said: "Follow me, follow me;"
And with laughter and song we went speeding along
By the shores of Life's beautiful sea.

Then we came to a valley more tropical far
  Than the wonderful vale of Cashmere,
And I saw from a bower a face like a flower
  Smile out on the gay Cavalier.
And he said: "We have come to humanity's goal:
  Here love and delight are intense."
But alas and alas! for the hopes of my soul—
  It was only the "Kingdom of Sense."

As I journeyed more slowly I met on the road
  A coach with retainers behind.
And they said: "Follow me, for our Lady's abode
  Belongs in that realm, you will find."
'Twas a grand dame of fashion, a newly-made bride,
  I followed, encouraged and bold;
But my hopes died away like the last gleams of
    day,
  For we came to the "Kingdom of Gold."

At the door of a cottage I asked a fair maid.
  "I have heard of that realm," she replied;
"But my feet never roam from the 'Kingdom of
    Home,'
  So I know not the way," and she sighed.
I looked on the cottage; how restful it seemed!
  And the maid was as fair as a dove.
Great light glorified my soul as I cried:
  "Why *home* is the 'Kingdom of Love!'"

UNDER THE SHEET.

WHAT a terrible night! Does the Night,
I wonder—
The Night, with her black veil down to
her feet
Like an ordained nun, know what lies
under
That awful, motionless, snow-white sheet?
The winds seem crazed, and, wildly howling,
Over the sad earth blindly go.
Do they and the dark clouds over them scowling,
Do they dream or know?

Why, here in the room, not a week or over—
Tho' it must be a week, not more than one—
(I cannot reckon of late or discover
When one day is ended or one begun),
But here in this room we were laughing lightly,
And glad was the measure our two hearts beat;
And the royal face that was smiling so brightly
Lies under that sheet.

I know not why—it is strange and fearful,
  But I am afraid of her, lying there;
She who was always so gay and cheerful,
  Lying so still with that stony stare:
She who was so like some grand sultana,
  Fond of color and glow and heat,
To lie there clothed in that awful manner
  In a stark white sheet.

She who was made out of summer blisses,
  Tropical, beautiful, gracious, fair,
To lie and stare at my fondest kisses—
  God! no wonder it whitens my hair.
Shriek, oh, wind! for the world is lonely;
  Trail cloud-veil to the nun Night's feet!
For all that I prized in life is only
  A shape and a sheet.

HIS YOUTH.

"DYING? I am not dying. Are you mad?
You think I need to ask for heavenly grace?
I think *you* are a fiend, who would be glad
To see me struggle in death's cold embrace.

"But, man, you lie! for I am strong—in truth
Stronger than I have been in years; and soon
I shall feel young again as in my youth,
My glorious youth—life's one great priceless boon.

"O youth, youth, youth! O God, that golden time,
When proud and glad I laughed the hours away.
Why, there's no sacrifice (perhaps no crime)
I'd pause at, could it make me young to-day.

"But I'm not *old!* I grew—just ill, somehow;
Grew stiff of limb, and weak, and dim of sight.
It was but sickness. I am better now,
Oh, vastly better, ever since last night.

"And I could weep warm floods of happy tears
To think my strength is coming back at last,

For I have dreamed of such an hour for years,
As I lay thinking of my glorious past.

"You shake your head? Why, man, if you were sane
I'd strike you to my feet, I would, in truth.
How dare you tell me that my hopes are vain?
How dare you say I have outlived my youth?

"'In heaven I may regain it?' Oh, be still!
I want no heaven but what my glad youth gave.
Its long, bright hours, its rapture and its thrill—
O youth, youth, youth! it is my *youth* I crave.

"There is no heaven! There's nothing but a deep
And yawning grave from which I shrink in fear.
I am not sure of even rest or sleep;
Perhaps we lie and *think*, as I have here.

"Think, think, think, think, as we lie there and rot,
And hear the young above us laugh in glee.
How dare you say I'm dying! *I am not.*
I would curse God if such a thing could be.

"Why, see me stand! why, hear this strong, full breath—
Dare you repeat that silly, base untruth?"
A cry—a fall—the silence known as death
Hushed his wild words. Well, has he found his youth?

WANTED—A LITTLE GIRL.

WHERE have they gone to—the little girls
With natural manners and natural curls;
Who love their dollies and like their toys,
And talk of something besides the boys?

Little old women in plenty I find,
Mature in manners and old of mind;
Little old flirts who talk of their "beaux,"
And vie with each other in stylish clothes.

Little old belles who, at nine and ten,
Are sick of pleasure and tired of men;
Weary of travel, of balls, of fun,
And find no new thing under the sun.

Once, in the beautiful long ago,
Some dear little children I used to know;
Girls who were merry as lambs at play,
And laughed and rollicked the livelong day.

They thought not at all of the "style" of their
clothes,
They never imagined that boys were "beaux"—
"Other girls' brothers" and "mates" were they;
Splendid fellows to help them play.

Where have they gone to? If you see
One of them anywhere send her to me.
I would give a medal of purest gold
To one of those dear little girls of old,
With an innocent heart and an open smile,
Who knows not the meaning of "flirt" or "style."

TWO SINNERS.

THERE was a man, it was said one time,
Who went astray in his youthful prime.
Can the brain keep cool and the heart keep quiet
When the blood is a river that's running riot?
And boys will be boys, the old folks say,
And a man is the better who's had his day.

The sinner reformed ; and the preacher told
Of the prodigal son who came back to the fold.
And Christian people threw open the door,
With a warmer welcome than ever before.
Wealth and honor were his to command,
And a spotless woman gave him her hand.

And the world strewed their pathway with blossoms abloom,
Crying, " God bless layde, and God bless groom !"

There was a maiden who went astray,
In the golden dawn of her life's young day.
She had more passion and heart than head,
And she followed blindly where fond Love led.
And Love unchecked is a dangerous guide
To wander at will by a fair girl's side.

The woman repented and turned from sin,
But no door opened to let her in.
The preacher prayed that she might be forgiven,
But told her to look for mercy—in heaven
For this is the law of the earth, we know :
That the woman is stoned, while the man may go.

A brave man wedded her after all,
But the world said, frowning, "We shall not call."

MEG'S CURSE.

THE sun rode high in a cloudless sky
Of a perfect summer morn.
She stood and gazed out into the street,
And wondered why she was born.
On the topmost branch of a maple-tree
That close by the window grew,
A robin called to his mate enthralled:
"I love but you, but you, but you."

A soft look came in her hardened face—
She had not wept for years;
But the robin's trill, as some sounds will,
Jarred open the door of tears.
She thought of the old home far away;
She heard the whir-r-r of the mill;
She heard the turtle's wild, sweet call,
And the wail of the whip-poor-will, whip-poor-will, whip-poor-will.

She saw again that dusty road
Whence he came riding down;
She smelled once more the flower she wore
In the breast of her simple gown.

Out on the new-mown meadow she heard
  Two blue-jays quarrel and fret,
And the warning cry of a Phœbe bird:
  "More wet, more wet, more wet."

With a blithe "hello" to the men below
  Who were spreading the new-mown hay,
The rider drew rein at her window-pane—
  How it all came back to-day!
How young she was, and how fair she was;
  What innocence crowned her brow!
The future seemed fair, for Love was there—
  And now—and now—and now.

In a dingy glass on the wall near by
  She gazed on her faded face.
"Well, Meg, I declare, what a beauty you are!"
  She sneered, "What an angel of grace!
Ha, ha, ha, ha, ha, ha, ha, ha!
  What a thing of beauty and grace!"
She reached out her arms with a moaning sob:
  "Oh, if I could go back!"
Then, swift and strange, came a sudden change;
  Her brow grew hard and black.

"A curse on the day and a curse on that man,
  And on all who are his," she cried.
"May he starve and be cold, may he live to be old
  When all who loved him have died."

Her wild voice frightened the robin away
  From the branch by the window-sill;
And little he knew as away he flew,
  Of the memories stirred by his trill.

He called to his mate on the grass below,
  "Follow me," as he soared on high;
And as mates have done since the world begun
  She followed, and asked not why.
The dingy room seemed curtained with gloom;
  Meg shivered with nameless dread.
The ghost of her youth and her murdered truth
  Seemed risen up from the dead.

She hurried out into the noisy street,
  For the silence made her afraid;
To flee from thought was all she sought,
  She cared not whither she strayed.
Still on she pressed in her wild unrest
  Up avenues skirting the park,
Where fashion's throng moved gayly along
  In Vanity Fair—when hark!

A clatter of hoofs down the stony street,
  The snort of a frightened horse
That was running wild, and a laughing child
  At play in its very course.
With one swift glance Meg saw it all.
  "*His* child—my God! *his* child!"

She cried aloud, as she rushed through the crowd
Like one grown suddenly wild.

There, almost under the iron feet,
Hemmed in by a passing cart,
Stood the baby boy—the pride and joy
Of the man who had broken her heart.
Past swooning women and shouting men
She fled like a flash of light;
With her slender arm she gathered from harm
The form of the laughing sprite.

The death-shod feet of the mad horse beat
Her down on the pavings gray;
But the baby laughed out with a merry shout,
And thought it splendid play.
He pulled her gown and called to her: "Say,
Dit up and do dat some more;
Das jus' ze way my papa play
Wiz me on ze nursery floor."

When the frightened father reached the scene,
His boy looked up and smiled
From the stiffening fold of the arm, death-cold,
Of Meg, who had died for his child.
Oh! idle words are a woman's curse
Who loves as woman can;
For put to the test, she will bare her breast
And die for the sake of the man.

A FABLE.

SOME cawing Crows, a hooting Owl,
A Hawk, a Canary, an old Marsh-Fowl,
One day all met together
To hold a caucus and settle the fate
Of a certain bird (without a mate),
A bird of another feather.

"My friends," said the Owl, with a look most wise,
"The Eagle is soaring too near the skies,
In a way that is quite improper;
Yet the world is praising her, so I'm told,
And I think her actions have grown so bold
That some of us ought to stop her."

"I have heard it said," quoth Hawk with a sigh,
"That young lambs died at the glance of her eye,
And I wholly scorn and despise her.
This and more, I am told, they say;
And I think that the only proper way
Is never to recognize her."

"I am quite convinced," said Crow with a caw,
"That the Eagle minds no moral law;
She's a most unruly creature."

"She's an ugly thing," piped Canary Bird ;
"Some call her handsome ; it's so absurd—
She hasn't a decent feature !"

Then the old Marsh Hen went hopping about ;
She said she was sure—she hadn't a doubt—
Of the truth of each bird's story ;
And she thought it her duty to stop her flight,
To pull her down from her lofty height,
And take the gilt from her glory.

But, lo ! from a peak on the mountain grand,
That looks out over the smiling land,
And over the mighty ocean,
The Eagle is spreading her splendid wings—
She rises, rises, and upward swings,
With a slow, majestic motion.

Up in the blue of God's own skies,
With a cry of rapture, away she flies,
Close to the Great Eternal.
She sweeps the world with her piercing sight ;
Her soul is filled with the Infinite
And the joy of things supernal.

Thus rise forever the chosen of God,
The genius-crowned or the power-shod,
Over the dust-world sailing ;
And back like splinters blown by the winds,
Must fall the missiles of silly minds,
Useless and unavailing.

THE WAY OF IT.

THIS is the way of it, wide world over,
One is beloved, and one is the lover,
One gives and the other receives.
One lavishes all in wild emotion,
One offers a smile for a life's devotion,
One hopes and the other believes.
One lies awake in the night to weep,
And the other drifts off in a sweet, sound sleep.

One soul is aflame with a godlike passion,
One plays with love in an idler's fashion,
One speaks and the other hears.
One sobs "I love you," and wet eyes show it,
And one laughs lightly, and says "I know it,"
With smiles for the other's tears.
One lives for the other and nothing beside,
And the other remembers the world is wide.

This is the way of it, sad earth over,
The heart that breaks is the heart of the lover,
And the other learns to forget.
"For what is the use of endless sorrow?
Though the sun goes down, it will rise to-morrow;
And life is not over yet."
Oh! I know this truth, if I know no other,
That passionate Love is Pain's own mother.

THE SUICIDE.

VAST was the wealth I carried in life's pack—
Youth, health, ambition, hope and trust; but Time
And Fate, those robbers fit for any crime,
Stole all, and left me but the empty sack.
Before me lay a long and lonely track
Of darkling hills and barren steeps to climb;
Behind me lay in shadows the sublime
Lost lands of Love's delight. Alack! Alack!

Unwearied, and with springing steps elate,
I had conveyed my wealth along the road.
The empty sack proved now a heavier load:
I was borne down beneath its worthless weight.
I stumbled on, and knocked at Death's dark gate.
There was no answer. Stung by sorrow's goad,
I *forced* my way into that grim abode,
And laughed, and flung Life's empty sack to Fate.

Unknown and uninvited I passed in
To that strange land that hangs between two goals,
Round which a dark and solemn river rolls—
More dread its silence than the loud earth's din.
And now, where was the peace I hoped to win?
Black-masted ships slid past me in great shoals,
Their bloody decks thronged with mistaken souls.
(God punishes mistakes sometimes like sin.)

Not rest and not oblivion I found.
My suffering self dwelt with me just the same;
But here no sleep was, and no sweet dreams came
To give me respite. Tyrant Death, uncrowned
By my own hand, still King of Terrors, frowned
Upon my shuddering soul, that shrank in shame
Before those eyes where sorrow blent with blame,
And those accusing lips that made no sound.

What gruesome shapes dawned on my startled sight!
What awful sighs broke on my listening ear!
The anguish of the earth, augmented here
A thousand-fold, made one continuous night.
The sack I flung away in impious spite
Hung yet upon me, filled, I saw in fear,

With tears that rained from earth's adjacent sphere,
And turned to stones in falling from that height.

And close about me pressed a grieving throng,
Each with his heavy sack, which bowed him so
His face was hidden. One of these mourned: "Know
Who enters here but finds the way more long
To those fair realms where sounds the angels' song.
There is no man-made exit out of woe;
Ye cannot dash the locked door down and go
To claim thy rightful joy through paths of wrong."

He passed into the shadows dim and gray,
And left me to pursue my path alone.
With terror greater than I yet had known.
Hard on my soul the awful knowledge lay,
Death had not ended life nor found God's way;
But, with my same sad sorrows still my own,
Where by-roads led to by-roads, thistle-sown,
I had but wandered off and gone astray.

With earth still near enough to hear its sighs,
With heaven afar and hell but just below,
Still on and on my lonely soul must go
Until I earn the right to Paradise.
We cannot force our way into God's skies,
Nor rush into the rest we long to know;
But patiently, with bleeding steps and slow,
Toil on to where selfhood in Godhood dies.

"NOW I LAY ME."

WHEN I pass from earth away,
Palsied though I be and gray,
May my spirit keep so young
That my failing, faltering tongue
Frames that prayer so dear to me,
Taught me at my mother's knee :
"*Now I lay me down to sleep,*"
(Passing to Eternal rest
On the loving parent breast)
"*I pray the Lord my soul to keep ;*"
(From all danger safe and calm
In the hollow of His palm ;)
"*If I should die before I wake,*"
(Drifting with a bated breath
Out of slumber into death,)
"*I pray the Lord my soul to take.*"
(From the body's claim set free
Sheltered in the Great to be.)
Simple prayer of trust and truth,
Taught me in my early youth—
Let my soul its beauty keep
When I lay me down to sleep.

THE MESSENGER.

SHE rose up in the early dawn,
And white and silently she moved
About the house. Four men had gone
To battle for the land they loved,
And she, the mother and the wife,
Waited for tidings from the strife.
How still the house seemed! and her tread
Was like the footsteps of the dead.

The long day passed; the dark night came.
She had not seen a human face.
Some voice spoke suddenly her name.
How loud it echoed in that place,
Where, day on day, no sound was heard
But her own footsteps. "Bring you word,'
She cried to whom she could not see,
"Word from the battle-plain to me?"

A soldier entered at the door,
And stood within the dim firelight:
"I bring you tidings of the four,"
He said, "who left you for the fight."

"God bless you, friend," she cried, "speak on!
For I can bear it. One is gone?"
"Ay, one is gone!" he said. "Which one?"
"Dear lady, he, your eldest son."

A deathly pallor shot across
  Her withered face; she did not weep.
She said: "It is a grievous loss,
  But God gives His belovèd sleep.
What of the living—of the three?
And when can they come back to me?"
The soldier turned away his head:
"Lady, your husband, too, is dead."

She put her hand upon her brow;
  A wild, sharp pain was in her eyes.
"My husband! Oh, God, help me now!"
  The soldier heard her shuddering sighs.
The task was harder than he thought.
"Your youngest son, dear madam, fought
Close at his father's side; both fell
Dead, by the bursting of a shell."

She moved her lips and seemed to moan.
  Her face had paled to ashen gray:
"Then one is left me—one alone,"
  She said, "of four who marched away.
Oh, overruling, All-wise God,
How can I pass beneath Thy rod!"
The soldier walked across the floor,
Paused at the window, at the door,

Wiped the cold dew-drops from his cheek
  And sought the mourner's side again.
"Once more, dear lady, I must speak:
  Your last remaining son was slain
Just at the closing of the fight,
'Twas he who sent me here to-night."
"God knows," the man said afterward,
"The fight itself was not so hard."

ILLOGICAL.

SHE stood beside me while I gave an order
for a bonnet.
She shuddered when I said, "And put a
bright bird's wing upon it."
A member of the Audubon Society was
she;
And cutting were her comments made on
worldly folks like me.

She spoke about the helpless birds we wickedly
were harming;
She quoted the statistics, and they really *were*
alarming;
She said God meant His little birds to sing in trees
and skies;
And there was pathos in her voice, and tears were
in her eyes.

"Oh, surely, in this beauteous world you can find
lovely things
Enough to trim your hats," she said, "without
the dear birds' wings."

I sat beside her that same day, in her own house at
dinner—
Angelic being that she was to entertain a sinner!

Her well-appointed table groaned beneath the
ample spread;
Course followed appetizing course, and hunger,
sated, fled.
But still my charming hostess urged: "Do have a
reed-bird, dear;
They are so delicate and sweet at this time of the
year."

A SERVIAN LEGEND.

LONG, long ago, ere yet our race began,
When earth was empty, waiting still for man,
Before the breath of life to him was given
The angels fell into a strife in heaven.

At length one furious demon grasped the sun
And sped away as fast as he could run,
And with a ringing laugh of fiendish mirth,
He leaped the battlements and fell to earth.

Dark was it then in heaven, but light below ;
For there the demon wandered to and fro,
Tilting aloft upon a slender pole
The orb of day—the pilfering old soul.

The angels wept and wailed ; but through the dark
The Great Creator's voice cried sternly : "Hark !
Who will restore to me the orb of Light,
Him will I honor in all heaven's sight."

Then over the battlements there dropped another.
(A shrewder angel well there could not be.)
Quoth he : " Behold my love for thee, my brother,
For I have left all heaven to stay with thee.

"Thy loneliness and wanderings I will share,
Thy heavy burden I will help thee bear."
"Well said," the demon answered, "and well
done,
But I'll not tax you with this heavy sun.

"Your company will cheer me, it is true,
And I could never think of burdening you."
Idly they wandered onward, side by side,
Till, by and by, they neared a silvery tide.

"Let's bathe," the angel suddenly suggested.
"Agreed," the demon answered. "I'll go last,
Because I needs must leave quite unmolested
This tiresome sun, which I will now make fast."

He set the pole well in the sandy turf,
And called a jackdaw near to watch the place.
Meanwhile the angel paddled in the surf,
And playfully dared his brother to a race.

They swam around together for awhile,
The demon always keeping near his prize,
Till presently the angel, with a smile,
Proposed a healthful diving exercise.

The demon hesitated. "But," thought he,
"The jackdaw will inform me with a cry
If this good brother tries deceiving me;
I will not be outdone by him—not I!"

Down, down they went. The angel in a trice
  Rose up again, and swift to shore he sped.
The jackdaw shrieked, but lo! a mile of ice
  The demon found had frozen o'er his head.

He swore an oath, and gathered all his force,
And broke the ice, to see the sun, of course,
Held firmly in the radiant angel's hand,
Who sailed away toward the heavenly land.

He gave pursuit. Wrath lent speed to his chase;
All heaven leaned down to watch the exciting
    race.
On, on they came, and still the Evil One
Gained on the angel burdened with the sun.

With bated breath and faces white as ghosts,
Over the walls leaned heaven's affrighted hosts.
Up, up, still up, the angel almost spent,
Threw one foot forward o'er the battlement.

The demon seized the other with a shout;
So fierce his clutch he pulled the bottom out,
As the good angel, fainting, laid the sun
Down by the throne of God, who cried: "Well
    done!
Thy great misfortune shall be made divine:
Man will I create with a foot like thine!"

PEEK-A-BOO.

THE cunningest thing that a baby can do
Is the very first time it plays peek-a-boo;

When it hides its pink little face in its hands,
And crows, and shows that it understands

What nurse, and mamma and papa, too,
Mean when they hide and cry, "Peek-a-boo, peek-a-boo."

Oh, what a wonderful thing it is,
When they find that baby can play like this;

And everyone listens, and thinks it true
That baby's gurgle means "Peek-a-boo, peek-a-boo";

And over and over the changes are rung
On the marvelous infant who talks so young.

I wonder if any one ever knew
A baby that never played peek-a-boo, peek-a-boo?

'Tis old as the hills are. I believe
Cain was taught it by Mother Eve;

For Cain was an innocent baby, too,
And I am sure he played peek-a-boo, peek-a-boo.

And the whole world full of the children of men,
Have all of them played that game since then.

Kings and princes and beggars, too,
Everyone has played peek-a-boo, peek-a-boo.

Thief and robber and ruffian bold,
The crazy tramp and the drunkard old,

All have been babies who laughed and knew
How to hide, and play peek-a-boo, peek-a-boo.

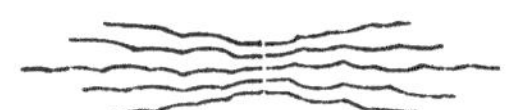

THE FALLING OF THRONES.

ABOVE the din of commerce, above the
clamor and rattle
Of labor disputing with riches, of Anarchists' threats and groans,
Above the hurry and hustle and roar of that
bloodless battle,
Where men are fighting for riches, I hear the falling of thrones.

I see no savage host, I hear no martial drumming,
But down in the dust at our feet lie the useless
crowns of kings;
And the mighty spirit of Progress is steadily coming, coming,
And the flag of one republic abroad to the world
he flings.

The Universal Republic, where worth not birth is
royal;
Where the lowliest born may climb on a self-made ladder to fame;
Where the highest and proudest born, if he be not
true and loyal,
Shall find no masking title to cover and gild his
shame.

Not with the bellow of guns and not with sabres
whetting,
But with growing minds of men is waged this
swordless fray;
While over the dim horizon the sun of royalty,
setting,
Lights, with a dying splendor, the humblest
toiler's way.

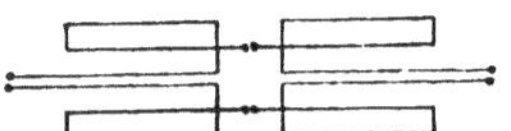

HER LAST LETTER.

SITTING alone by the window,
Watching the moonlit street,
Bending my head to listen
To the well-known sound of your feet,
I have been wondering, darling,
How I can bear the pain,
When I watch, with sighs and tear-wet eyes,
And wait for your coming in vain.

For I know that a day approaches
When your heart will tire of me;
When by door and gate I may watch and wait
For a form I shall not see.
When the love that is now my heaven,
The kisses that make my life,
You will bestow on another,
And that other will be—your wife.

You will grow weary of sinning
(Though you do not call it so),
You will long for a love that is purer
Than the love that we two know.
God knows I have loved you dearly,
With a passion strong as true;
But you will grow tired and leave me,
Though I gave up all for you.

I was as pure as the morning
  When I first looked on your face ;
I knew I never could reach you
  In your high, exalted place.
But I looked and loved and worshiped
  As a flower might worship a star,
And your eyes shone down upon me,
  And you seemed so far—so far.

And then? Well, then, you loved me,
  Loved me with all your heart;
But we could not stand at the altar,
  We were so far apart.
If a star should wed with a flower
  The star must drop from the sky,
Or the flower in trying to reach it
  Would droop on its stalk and die.

But you said that you loved me, darling,
  And swore by the heavens above
That the Lord and all of His angels
  Would sanction and bless our love.
And I? I was weak, not wicked.
  My love was as pure as true,
And sin itself seemed a virtue
  If only shared by you.

We have been happy together,
  Though under the cloud of sin,
But I know that the day approaches
  When my chastening must begin.

You have been faithful and tender,
  But you will not always be,
And I think I had better leave you
  While your thoughts are kind of me.

I know my beauty is fading—
  Sin furrows the fairest brow—
And I know that your heart will weary
  Of the face you smile on now.
You will take a bride to your bosom
  After you turn from me ;
You will sit with your wife in the moonlight,
  And hold her babe on your knee.

Oh, God ! I never could bear it ;
  It would madden my brain, I know ;
And so while you love me dearly
  I think I had better go.
It is sweeter to feel, my darling—
  To know as I fall asleep—
That some one will mourn me and miss me,
  That some one is left to weep,

Than to die as I should in the future,
  To drop in the street some day,
Unknown, unwept and forgotten
  After you cast me away.
Perhaps the blood of the Saviour
  Can wash my garments clean ;
Perchance I may drink of the waters
  That flow through pastures green.

Perchance we may meet in heaven,
  And walk in the streets above,
With nothing to grieve us or part us
  Since our sinning was all through love.
God says, "Love one another,"
  And down to the depths of hell
Will he send the soul of a women
  Because she loved—and fell?

* * * * * *

And so in the moonlight he found her,
  Or found her beautiful clay,
Lifeless and pallid as marble,
  For the spirit had flown away.
The farewell words she had written
  She held to her cold, white breast,
And the buried blade of a dagger
  Told how she had gone to rest.

BABYLAND.

HAVE you heard of the Valley of Babyland,
The realm where the dear little darlings stay,
Till the kind storks go, as all men know,
And oh, so tenderly bring them away?
The paths are winding and past all finding
By all save the storks, who understand
The gates and the highways and the intricate by-ways
That lead to Babyland.

All over the Valley of Babyland
Sweet flowers bloom in the soft green moss,
And under the ferns fair, and under the plants there
Lie little heads like spools of floss.
With a soothing number the river of slumber
Flows o'er a bedway of silver sand;
And angels are keeping watch o'er the sleeping
Babes of Babyland.

The path to the Valley of Babyland
Only the kingly, kind storks know;
If they fly over mountains, or wade through fountains,

No man sees them come or go.
But an angel maybe, who guards some baby,
Or a fairy, perhaps, with her magic wand,
Brings them straightway to the wonderful gateway
That leads to Babyland.

And there, in the Valley of Babyland,
Under the mosses and leaves and ferns,
Like an unfledged starling they find the darling
For whom the heart of a mother yearns ;
And they lift him lightly and snug him tightly
In feathers soft as a lady's hand,
And off with a rockaway step they walk away
Out of Babyland.

As they go from the Valley of Babyland
Forth into the world of great unrest,
Sometimes weeping he wakes from sleeping
Before he reaches the mother's breast.
Ah, how she blesses him, how she caresses him,
Bonniest bird in the bright home band
That o'er land and water the kind stork brought her
From far-off Babyland.

FISHING.

MAYBE this is fun, sitting in the sun,
With a book and parasol, as my angler wishes,
While he dips his line in the ocean brine,
Under the impression that his bait will catch the fishes.

'Tis romantic—yes, but I must confess
Thoughts of shady rooms at home somehow seem more inviting.
But I dare not move—"Quiet there, my love!"
Says my angler, "for I think a monster fish is biting."

Oh, of course, it's bliss—but how hot it is!
And the rock I'm sitting on grows harder every minute;
Still my fisher waits, trying various baits,
But the basket at his side, I see, has nothing in it.

Oh, it's just the way to pass a July day,
Arcadian and sentimental, dreamy, idle, charming;
But how fierce the sunlight falls! and the way that insect crawls
Along my neck and down my back is really quite alarming.

"Any luck?" I gently ask of the angler at his task;
"There's something pulling at my line," he says;
"I've almost caught it."
But when, with blistered face, we our homeward steps retrace,
We take the little basket just as empty as we brought it.

THE OLD STAGE QUEEN.

BACK in her box by the curtains shaded
She sits alone, by the house unseen ;
Her eye is dim and her cheek is faded,
She who once was the people's queen.

The curtain rolls up, and she sees before her
A vision of beauty and youth and grace.
Ah ! no wonder all hearts adore her,
Silver-throated and fair of face.

Out of her box she leans and listens :
O ! is it with pleasure or with despair
That her thin cheek pales, and her dim eye glistens
While that fresh young voice sings the grand old air ?

She is back again in her past's bright splendor,
When life was worth living and love was a truth ;
Ere Time had told her she must surrender
Her double dower of fame and youth.

It is she herself who stands there singing
To that sea of faces, that shines and stirs ;
And the cheers on cheers that go up ringing
And rousing the echoes, are hers, all hers !

Just for one moment the sweet delusion
  Quickens her pulses, and blurs her sight,
And wakes within her that wild confusion
  Of joy that is anguish and fierce delight.

Then the curtain goes down, and the lights are gleaming
  Brightly o'er circle and box and stall ;
She starts like a sleeper who wakes from dreaming:
  Her youth lies under Time's funeral pall.

Her day is dead, and her star descended
  Never to rise or to shine again ;
Her reign is over, her queenship ended—
  A new name is sounded and sung by men

All the glitter and glow and splendor,
  All the glory of that lost day,
With the friends that seemed true and the love that seemed tender,
  Why, what is it all but a dead bouquet !

She rises to go ; has the night turned colder?
  The new queen answers to call and shout ;
And the old queen looks back over her shoulder
  As, all unnoticed, she passes out.

THE PRINCESS'S FINGER-NAIL.

A TALE OF NONSENSE LAND.

ALL through the Castle of High-bred Ease,
Where the chief employment was do-as-you-please,
Spread consternation and wild despair.
The queen was wringing her hands and hair;
The maids of honor were sad and solemn;
The pages looked blank as they stood in column;
The court-jester blubbered, "Boo-hoo, boo-hoo";
The cook in the kitchen dropped tears in the stew;
And all through the castle went sob and wail,
For the princess had broken her finger-nail:
The beautiful Princess Red-as-a-Rose,
Bride-elect of the Lord High-Nose,
Broken her finger-nail down to the quick—
No wonder the queen and her court were sick.
Never sorrow so dread before
Had dared to enter that castle door.
Oh! what would my Lord His-High-Nose say
When she took off her glove on her wedding-day?
The fairest princess in Nonsense Land,
With a broken finger-nail on her hand!
'Twas a terrible, terrible accident,

And they called a meeting of parliament ;
And never before that royal Court
Had come such question of grave import
As "How could you hurry a nail to grow?"
And the skill of the kingdom was called to show.
They sent for Monsieur File-'em-off ;
He smoothed down the corners so ragged and
rough.
They sent for Madame la Diamond-Dust,
Who lived on the fingers of upper-crust ;
They sent for Professor de Chamois-Skin,
Who took her powder and rubbed it in ;
They sent for the pudgy nurse Fat-on-the-bone
To bathe her finger in eau de Cologne ;
And they called the Court surgeon, Monsieur Red-
Tape,
To hear what he thought of the new nail's shape.
Over the kingdom the telegrams flew
Which told how the finger-nail thrived and grew ;
And all through the realm of Nonsense Land
They offered up prayers for the princess's hand.
At length the glad tidings were heard with a
shout
That the princess's finger-nail had grown out:
Pointed and polished and pink and clean,
Befitting the hand of a some-day queen.
Salutes were fired all over the land
By the home-guard battery pop-gun band;
And great was the joy of my Lord High-Nose,
Who straightway ordered his wedding clothes,

And paid his tailor, Don Wait-for-aye,
Who died of amazement the self-same day.
My lord by a jury was judged insane;
For they said, and the truth of the saying was
plain,
That a lord of such very high pedigree
Would never be paying his bills, you see,
Unless he was out of his head; and so
They locked him up without more ado.
And the beautiful Princess Red-as-a-Rose
Pined for her lover, my Lord High-Nose,
Till she entered a convent and took the veil—
And this is the end of my nonsense tale.

A BABY IN THE HOUSE.

I KNEW that a baby was hid in the house;
Though I saw no cradle and heard no cry,
But the husband went tiptoeing 'round like a mouse,
And the good wife was humming a soft lullaby;
And there was a look on the face of that mother
That I knew could mean only *one* thing, and no other.

"The *mother*," I said to myself; for I knew
That the woman before me was certainly that,
For there lay in the corner a tiny cloth shoe,
And I saw on the stand such a wee little hat;
And the beard of the husband said plain as could be,
"Two fat, chubby hands have been tugging at me."

And he took from his pocket a gay picture-book,
And a dog that would bark if you pulled on a string;
And the wife laid them up with such a pleased look;
And I said to myself, "There is no other thing
But a babe that could bring about all this, and so
That one is in hiding here somewhere, I know."

I stayed but a moment, and saw nothing more,
  And heard not a sound, yet I knew I was right;
What else could the shoe mean that lay on the floor,
  The book and the toy, and the faces so bright?
And what made the husband as still as a mouse?
I am sure, *very* sure, there's a babe in that house.

THE FOOLISH ELM.

THE bold young Autumn came riding along
One day where an elm-tree grew.
"You are fair," he said, as she bent down her head,
"Too fair for your robe's dull hue.
You are far too young for a garb so old;
Your beauty needs color and sheen.
Oh, I would clothe you in scarlet and gold
Befitting the grace of a queen.

"For one little kiss on your lips, sweet elm,
For one little kiss, no more,
I would give you, I swear, a robe more fair
Than ever a princess wore.
One little kiss on those lips, my pet,
And lo! you shall stand, I say,
Queen of the forest, and, better yet,
Queen of my heart alway."

She tossed her head, but he took the kiss—
'Tis the way of lovers bold—
And a gorgeous dress for that sweet caress
He gave ere the morning was old.

For a week and a day she ruled a queen
  In beauty and splendid attire ;
For a week and a day she was loved, I ween,
  With the love that is born of desire.

Then bold-eyed Autumn went on his way
  In search of a tree more fair ;
And mob winds tattered her garments and scattered
  Her finery here and there.
Poor and faded and ragged and cold
  She rocked in her wild distress,
And longed for the dull green gown she had sold
  For her fickle lover's caress.

And the days went by and Winter came,
  And his tyrannous tempests beat
On the shivering tree, whose robes of flame
  He had trampled under his feet.
I saw her reach up to the mocking skies
  Her poor arms, bare and thin ;
Ah, well-a-day ! it is ever the way
  With a woman who trades with sin.

ROBIN'S MISTAKE.

WHAT do you think Red Robin
Found by a mow of hay?
Why, a flask brimful of liquor,
That the mowers brought that day
To slake their thirst in the hayfield.
And Robin he shook his head:
"Now, I wonder what they call it,
And how it tastes?" he said.

"I have seen the mowers drink it—
Why isn't it good for me?
So I'll just draw out the stopper
And get at the stuff, and see!"
But alas! for the curious Robin,
One draught, and he burned his throat
From his bill to his poor crop's lining,
And he could not utter a note.

And his head grew light and dizzy,
And he staggered left and right,
Tipped over the flask of brandy,
And spilled it, every mite.

But after awhile he sobered,
  And quietly flew away,
And he never has tasted liquor,
  Or touched it, since that day.

But I heard him say to his kindred,
  In the course of a friendly chat,
"These men think they are above us,
  Yet they drink such stuff as that!
Oh, the poor degraded creatures!
  I am glad I am only a bird!"
Then he flew up over the meadow,
  And that was all I heard.

NEW YEAR RESOLVE.

AS the dead year is clasped by a dead December,
So let your dead sins with your dead days lie.
A new life is yours and a new hope. Remember
We build our own ladders to climb to the sky.

Stand out in the sunlight of promise, forgetting
Whatever the past held of sorrow and wrong.
We waste half our strength in a useless regretting;
We sit by old tombs in the dark too long.

Have you missed in your aim? Well, the mark is still shining.
Did you faint in the race? Well, take breath for the next.
Did the clouds drive you back? But see yonder their lining.
Were you tempted and fell? Let it serve for a text.

As each year hurries by, let it join that procession
  Of skeleton shapes that march down to the past
While you take your place in the line of progression,
  With your eyes to the heavens, your face to the blast.

I tell you the future can hold no terrors
  For any sad soul while the stars revolve,
If he will stand firm on the grave of his errors,
  And instead of regretting—resolve, resolve!

It is never too late to begin rebuilding,
  Though all into ruins your life seems hurled;
For see! how the light of the New Year is gilding
  The wan, worn face of the bruised old world.

WHAT WE WANT.

ALL hail the dawn of a new day breaking,
When a strong-armed nation shall take away
The weary burdens from backs that are aching
With maximum labor and minimum pay;
When no man is honored who hoards his millions;
When no man feasts on another's toil.
And God's poor suffering, striving billions
Shall share his riches of sun and soil.

There is gold for all in the earth's broad bosom,
There is food for all in the land's great store;
Enough is provided if rightly divided;
Let each man take what he needs—no more.
Shame on the miser with unused riches,
Who robs the toiler to swell his hoard,
Who beats down the wage of the digger of ditches,
And steals the bread from the poor man's board.

Shame on the owner of mines whose cruel
And selfish measures have brought him wealth,
While the ragged wretches who dig his fuel
Are robbed of comfort and hope and health.

Shame on the ruler who rides in his carriage
  Bought with the labor of half-paid men—
Men who are shut out of home and marriage
  And are herded like sheep in a hovel pen.

Let the clarion voice of the nation wake him
  To broader vision and fairer play;
Or let the hand of a just law shake him
  Till his ill-gained dollars shall roll away.
Let no man dwell under a mountain of plunder,
  Let no man suffer with want and cold;
We want right living, not mere alms-giving;
  We want just dividing of labor and gold.

THE TWO GLASSES.

THERE sat two glasses, filled to the brim,
On a rich man's table, rim to rim.
One was ruddy and red as blood,
And one was as clear as the crystal flood.

Said the glass of wine to his paler brother:
"Let us tell tales of the past to each other.
I can tell of banquet, and revel, and mirth,
Where I was king, for I ruled in might;
And the proudest and grandest souls on earth
Fell under my touch, as though struck with blight.
From the heads of kings I have torn the crown;
From the heights of fame I have hurled men down;
I have blasted many an honored name;
I have taken virtue and given shame;
I have tempted the youth, with a sip, a taste,
That has made his future a barren waste.
Far greater than any king am I,
Or than any army under the sky.
I have made the arm of the driver fail,
And sent the train from its iron rail.
I have made good ships go down at sea,
And the shrieks of the lost were sweet to me.
Fame, strength, wealth, genius, before me fall,
And my might and power are over all.
Ho! ho! pale brother," laughed the wine,
"Can you boast of deeds as great as mine?"

Said the glass of water: "I cannot boast
Of a king dethroned or a murdered host;
But I can tell of hearts that were sad,
By my crystal drops made light and glad.
Of thirsts I have quenched, and brows I have laved;
Of hands I have cooled and souls I have saved.
I have leaped through the valley and dashed down the mountain;
Slept in the sunshine and dripped from the fountain.
I have burst my cloud-fetters and dropped from the sky,
And everywhere gladdened the landscape and eye.
I have eased the hot forehead of fever and pain;
I have made the parched meadows grow fertile with grain;
I can tell of the powerful wheel o' the mill,
That ground out the flour and turned at my will;
I can tell of manhood, debased by you,
That I have uplifted and crowned anew.
I cheer, I help, I strengthen and aid,
I gladden the heart of man and maid;
I set the chained wine-captive free,
And all are better for knowing me."

These are the tales they told each other,
The glass of wine, and its paler brother,
As they sat together, filled to the brim,
On the rich man's table, rim to rim.

A PIN.

OH, I know a certain woman who is reckoned with the good,
But she fills me with more terror than a raging lion could.
The little chills run up and down my spine whene'er we meet,
Though she seems a gentle creature and she's very trim and neat.

And she has a thousand virtues and not one acknowledged sin,
But she is the sort of person you could liken to a pin.
And she pricks you, and she sticks you, in a way that can't be said—
When you seek for what has hurt you, why, you cannot find the head.

But she fills you with discomfort and exasperating pain—
If anybody asks you why, you really can't explain.
A pin is such a tiny thing—of that there is no doubt—
Yet when it's sticking in your flesh, you're wretched till it's out!

She is wonderfully observing. When she meets a pretty girl
She is always sure to tell her if her " bang " is out of curl.
And she is so sympathetic; to her friend who's much admired,
She is often heard remarking: " Dear, you look so *worn* and tired!"

And she is a careful critic; for on yesterday she eyed
The new dress I was airing with a woman's natural pride,
And she said: "Oh, how becoming!" and then softly added, "It
Is really a misfortune that the basque is such a fit."

Then she said: "If you had heard me yestereve, I'm sure, my friend,
You would say I am a champion who knows how to defend."
And she left me with a feeling—most unpleasant, I aver—
That the whole world would despise me if it hadn't been for her.

Whenever I encounter her, in such a nameless way
She gives me the impression I am at my worst that day;

And the hat that was imported (and that cost me
half a sonnet)
With just one glance from her round eyes becomes
a Bowery bonnet.

She is always bright and smiling, sharp and shining
for a thrust;
Use does not seem to blunt her point, nor does she
gather rust.
Oh! I wish some hapless specimen of mankind
would begin
To tidy up the world for me, by picking up this
pin.

BREAKING THE DAY IN TWO.

WHEN from dawn till noon seems one long
day,
And from noon till night another,
Oh, then should a little boy come from
play,
And creep into the arms of his mother.
Snugly creep and fall asleep,
O come, my baby, do;
Creep into my lap, and with a nap,
We'll break the day in two.

When the shadows slant for afternoon,
When the midday meal is over;
When the winds have sung themselves into a
swoon,
And the bees drone in the clover.
Then hie to me, hie, for a lullaby—
Come, my baby, do;
Creep into my lap, and with a nap
We'll break the day in two.

We'll break it in two with a crooning song,
  With a soft and soothing number;
For the day has no right to be so long
  And keep my baby from slumber.
Then rock-a-by, rock, may white dreams flock
  Like angels over you;
Baby's gone, and the deed is done
  We've broken the day in two.

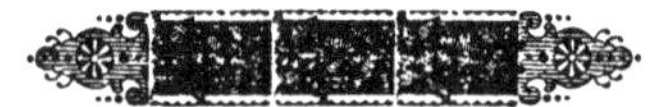

THE RAPE OF THE MIST.

HIGH o'er the clouds a Sunbeam shone,
And far down under him,
With a subtle grace that was all her own,
The Mist gleamed, fair and dim.

He looked at her with his burning eyes
And longed to fall at her feet;
Of all sweet things there under the skies,
He thought her the thing most sweet.

He had wooed oft, as a sunbeam may,
Wave, and blossom, and flower;
But never before had he felt the sway
Of a great love's mighty power.

Tall cloud-mountains and vast space-seas,
Wind, and tempest, and fire—
What are obstacles such as these
To a heart that is filled with desire?

Boldly he trod over cloud and star,
Boldly he swam through space,
She caught the glow of his eyes afar
And veiled her delicate face.

He was so strong and he was so bright,
  And his breath was a breath of flame ;
The Mist grew pale with a vague, strange fright,
  As fond, yet fierce, he came.

Close to his heart she was clasped and kissed ;
  She swooned in love's alarms,
And dead lay the beautiful pale-faced Mist
  In the Sunbeam's passionate arms.

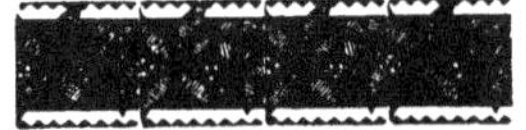

THE MANIAC.

I SAW them sitting in the shade ;
The long green vines hung over,
But could not hide the gold-haired maid
And Earl, my dark-eyed lover.
His arm was clasped so close, so close,
Her eyes were softly lifted,
While his eyes drank the cheek of rose
And breasts like snowflakes drifted.

A strange noise sounded in my brain ;
I was a guest unbidden.
I stole away, but came again
With two knives snugly hidden.
I stood behind them. Close they kissed,
While eye to eye was speaking ;
I aimed my steels, and neither missed
The heart I sent it seeking.

There were two death-shrieks mingled so
It seemed like one voice crying.
I laughed—it was such bliss, you know,
To hear and see them dying.

I laughed and shouted while I stood
  Above the lovers, gazing
Upon the trickling rills of blood
  And frightened eyes fast glazing.

It was such joy to see the rose
  Fade from her cheek forever ;
To know the lips he kissed so close
  Could answer never, never.
To see his arm grow stark and cold,
  And know it could not hold her ;
To know that while the world grew old
  His eyes could not behold her.

A crowd of people thronged about,
  Brought thither by my laughter ;
I gave one last triumphant shout—
  Then darkness followed after.
That was a thousand years ago ;
  Each hour I live it over,
For there, just out of reach, you know,
  She lies, with Earl, my lover.

They lie there, staring, staring so
  With great, glazed eyes to taunt me.
Will no one bury them down low,
  Where they shall cease to haunt me ?
He kissed her lips, not mine ; the flowers
  And vines hung all about them.
Sometimes I sit and laugh for hours
  To think just how I found them.

And then I sometimes stand and shriek
  In agony of terror :
I see the red warm in her cheek,
  Then laugh loud at my error.
My cheek was all too pale, he thought ;
  He deemed hers far the brightest.
Ha ! but my dagger touched a spot
  That made *her* face the whitest !

But oh, the days seem very long,
  Without my Earl, my lover ;
And something in my head seems wrong
  The more I think it over.
Ah ! look—she is not dead—look there !
  She's standing close beside me !
Her eyes are open—how they stare !
  Oh, hide me ! hide me ! hide me !

WHAT IS FLIRTATION?

WHAT is flirtation? Really,
How can I tell you that?
But when she smiles I see its wiles,
And when he lifts his hat.

'Tis walking in the moonlight,
'Tis buttoning on a glove,
'Tis lips that speak of plays next week,
While eyes are talking love.

Tis meeting in the ball-room,
'Tis whirling in the dance;
'Tis something hid beneath the lid,
More than a simple glance.

'Tis lingering in the hallway,
'Tis sitting on the stair,
'Tis bearded lips on finger-tips,
If mamma isn't there.

'Tis tucking in the carriage,
'Tis asking for a call;
'Tis long good-nights in tender lights,
And that is—no, not all!

'Tis parting when it's over,
And one goes home to sleep;
Best joys must end, tra la, my friend,
But one goes home to weep!

HOW DOES LOVE SPEAK?

HOW does Love speak?
In the faint flush upon the tell-tale cheek,
And in the pallor that succeeds it; by
The quivering lid of an averted eye—
The smile that proves the parent of a sigh:
Thus doth Love speak.

How does Love speak?
By the uneven heart-throbs, and the freak
Of bounding pulses that stand still and ache,
While new emotions, like strange barges, make
Along vein-channels their disturbing course,
Still as the dawn, and with the dawn's swift force:
Thus doth Love speak.

How does Love speak?
In the avoidance of that which we seek—
The sudden silence and reserve when near;
The eye that glistens with an unshed tear;
The joy that seems the counterpart of fear,
As the alarmèd heart leaps in the breast,
And knows, and names, and greets its godlike guest:
Thus doth Love speak.

How does Love speak?
In the proud spirit suddenly grown meek,
The haughty heart grown humble; in the tender
And unnamed light that floods the world with
splendor;
In the resemblance which the fond eyes trace
In all fair things to one beloved face;
In the shy touch of hands that thrill and tremble;
In looks and lips that can no more dissemble:
Thus doth Love speak.

How does Love speak?
In wild words that uttered seem so weak
They shrink ashamed to silence; in the fire
Glance strikes with glance, swift flashing high and
higher,
Like lightnings that precede the mighty storm;
In the deep, soulful stillness; in the warm,
Impassioned tide that sweeps thro' throbbing veins,
Between the shores of keen delights and pains;
In the embrace where madness melts in bliss,
And in the convulsive rapture of a kiss:
Thus doth Love speak.

AS YOU GO THROUGH LIFE.

DON'T look for the flaws as you go through
life;
And even when you find them,
It is wise and kind to be somewhat blind
And look for the virtue behind them.
For the cloudiest night has a hint of light
Somewhere in its shadows hiding;
It is better by far to hunt for a star,
Than the spots on the sun abiding.

The current of life runs ever away
To the bosom of God's great ocean.
Don't set your force 'gainst the river's course
And think to alter its motion.
Don't waste a curse on the universe—
Remember it lived before you.
Don't butt at the storm with your puny form,
But bend and let it go o'er you.

The world will never adjust itself
To suit your whims to the letter.
Some things must go wrong your whole life long,
And the sooner you know it the better.
It is folly to fight with the Infinite,
And go under at last in the wrestle;
The wiser man shapes into God's plan
As water shapes into a vessel.

MEMORY'S RIVER.

IN Nature's bright blossoms not always re-
poses
That strange subtle essence more rare
than their bloom,
Which lies in the hearts of carnations and
roses,
That unexplained something by men called per·
fume.
Though modest the flower, yet great is its power
And pregnant with meaning each pistil and leaf,
If only it hides there, if only abides there,
The fragrance suggestive of love, joy and grief.

Not always the air that a master composes
Can stir human heart-strings with pleasure or
pain.
But strange, subtle chords, like the scent of the
roses,
Breathe out of some measures, though simple the
strain.
And lo ! when you hear them, you love them and
fear them,
You tremble with anguish, you thrill with de-
light,

For back of them slumber old dreams without number,
And faces long vanished peer out into sight.

Those dear foolish days when the earth seemed all beauty,
Before you had knowledge enough to be sad;
When youth held no higher ideal of duty
Than just to lilt on through the world and be glad.
On harmony's river they seemed to float hither
With all the sweet fancies that hung round that time—
Life's burdens and troubles turn into air-bubbles
And break on the music's swift current of rhyme.

Fair Folly comes back with her spell while you listen
And points to the paths where she led you of old.
You gaze on past sunsets, you see dead stars glisten,
You bathe in life's glory, you swoon in death's cold.
All pains and all pleasures surge up through those measures,
Your heart is wrenched open with earthquakes of sound;
From ashes and embers rise Junes and Decembers,
Lost islands in fathoms of feeling refound.

Some airs are like outlets of memory's oceans,
They rise in the past and flow into the heart;
And down them float shipwrecks of mighty emotions,
All sea-soaked and storm-tossed and drifting apart:
Their fair timbers battered, their lordly sails tattered,
Their skeleton crew of dead days on their decks;
Then a crash of chords blending, a crisis, an ending—
The music is over, and vanished the wrecks.

THE LADY AND THE DAME.

SO thou hast the art, good dame, thou swearest,
To keep Time's perishing touch at bay
From the roseate splendor of the cheek so tender,
And the silver threads from the gold away;
And the tell-tale years that have hurried by us
Shall tiptoe back, and, with kind good-will,
They shall take their traces from off our faces,
If we will trust to thy magic skill.

Thou speakest fairly ; but if I listen
And buy thy secret and prove its truth,
Hast thou the potion and magic lotion
To give me also the *heart* of youth ?
With the cheek of rose and the eye of beauty,
And the lustrous locks of life's lost prime,
Wilt thou bring thronging each hope and longing
That made the glory of that dead Time ?

When the sap in the trees sets young buds bursting,
And the song of the birds fills the air like spray,
Will rivers of feeling come once more stealing
From the beautiful hills of the far-away ?

Wilt thou demolish the tower of reason
  And fling forever down into the dust,
The caution time brought me, the lessons life taught me,
  And put in their places my old sweet trust?

If Time's footprint from my brow is driven,
  Canst thou, too, take with thy subtle powers
The burden of thinking, and let me go drinking
  The careless pleasures of youth's bright hours?
If silver threads from my tresses vanish,
  If a glow once more in my pale cheek gleams,
Wilt thou slay duty and give back the beauty
  Of days untroubled by aught but dreams?

When the soft, fair arms of the siren Summer
  Encircle the earth in their languorous fold,
Will vast, deep oceans of sweet emotions
  Surge through my veins as they surged of old?
Canst thou bring back from a day long vanished
  The leaping pulse and the boundless aim?
I will pay thee double for all thy trouble,
  If thou wilt restore all these, good dame.

A MARRIED COQUETTE

SIT still, I say, and dispense with heroics !
I hurt your wrists ? Well, you have hurt me.
It is time you found out that all men are not stoics,
Nor toys to be used as your mood may be.
I will not let go of your hands, nor leave you
Until I have spoken. No man, you say,
Dared ever so treat you before ? I believe you,
For you have dealt only with *boys* till to-day.

You women lay stress on your fine perception,
Your intuitions are prated about ;
You claim an occult sort of conception
Of matters which men must reason out.
So then, of course, when you asked me kindly
"To call again soon," you read my heart.
I cannot believe you were acting blindly ;
You saw my passion for you from the start.

You are one of those women who charm without trying ;
The clay you are made of is magnet ore,
And I am the steel ; yet, there's no denying
You led me to loving you more and more.

You are fanning a flame that may burn too brightly,
  Oft easily kindled, but hard to put out ;
I am not a man to be played with lightly,
  To come at a gesture and go at a pout.

A brute you call me, a creature inhuman ;
  You say I insult you, and bid me go.
And you ? Oh, you are a saintly woman,
  With thoughts as pure as the drifted snow.
Pah ! you are but one of a thousand beauties
  Who think they are living exemplary lives.
They break no commandments, and do all their duties
  As Christian women and spotless wives.

But with drooping of lids, and lifting of faces,
  And baring of shoulders, and well-timed sighs,
And the devil knows what other subtle graces,
  You are mental wantons, who sin with the eyes.
You lure love to wake, yet bid it keep under,
  You tempt us to fall, but bid reason control ;
And then you are full of an outraged wonder
  When we get to wanting you, body and soul.

Why, look at yourself ! You were no stranger
  To the fact that my heart was already on fire.
When you asked me to call you knew my danger,
  Yet here you are, dressed in the gown I admire ;
For half of the evil on earth is invented
  By vain, pretty women with nothing to do

But to keep themselves manicured, powdered and scented,
And seek for sensations amusing and new.

But when I play at love at a lady's commanding,
I always am certain to win one game;
So there—there—there! I will leave my branding
On the lips that are free now to cry "Shame, shame!"
You hate me? Quite likely! It does not surprise me.
Brute force? I confess it; *but still you were kissed;*
And one thing is certain—you cannot despise me
For having been played with, controlled, and dismissed.

And the next time you see that a man is attracted
By the beauty and graces that are not for him,
Don't lead him on to be half distracted;
Keep out of deep waters although you can swim.
For when he is caught in the whirlpool of passion,
Where many bold swimmers are seen to drown,
A man will reach out and, in desperate fashion,
Will drag whoever is nearest him down.

Though the strings of his heart may be wrenched and riven
By a maiden coquette who has led him along,
She can be pardoned, excused and forgiven,
For innocence blindfolded walks into wrong.

But she who has willingly taken the fetter
  That Cupid forges at Hymen's command—
Well, she is the woman who ought to know better;
  She needs no mercy at any man's hand.

In the game of hearts, though a woman be winner,
  The odds are ever against her, you know ;
The world is ready to call her a sinner,
  And man is ready to make her so.
Shame is likely, and sorrow is certain,
  And the man has the best of it, end as it may.
So now, my lady, we'll drop the curtain,
  And put out the lights. We are through with
    our play.

A PLEA.

COLUMBIA, large-hearted and tender,
Too long for the good of your kin
You have shared your home's comfort and splendor
With all who have asked to come in.
The smile of your true eyes has lighted
The way to your wide-open door;
You have held out full hands and invited
The beggar to take from your store.

Your overrun proud sister nations,
Whose offspring you help them to keep,
Are sending their poorest relations—
Their unruly, vicious black sheep.
Unwashed and unlettered you take them,
And lo! we are pushed from your knee;
We are governed by laws as *they* make them,
We are slaves in the land of the free.

Columbia, you know the devotion
Of those who have sprung from your soil.
Shall aliens born over the ocean
Dispute us the fruits of our toil?

Most noble and gracious of mothers,
  Your children rise up and demand
That you bring us no more foster-brothers
  To breed discontent in the land.

Be prudent before you are zealous—
  Not generous only, but just ;
Our hearts are grown wrathful and jealous
  Toward those who have outraged your trust.
They jostle and crowd in our places,
  They sneer at the comforts you gave ;
We say, shut the door in their faces
  Until they have learned to behave.

In hearts that are greedy and hateful,
  They harbor ill-will and deceit ;
They ask for more favors, ungrateful
  For those you have poured at their feet.
Rise up in your grandeur, and straightway
  Bar out the bold, clamoring mass ;
Let sentinels stand at your gateway,
  To see who is worthy to pass.

Give first to your own faithful toilers
  The freedom our birthright should claim,
And take from these ruthless despoilers
  The power which they use to our shame.
Columbia, too long you have dallied
  With foes whom you feed from your store ;
It is time that your wardens were rallied
  And stationed outside the locked door.

THE SUMMER GIRL.

SHE'S the jauntiest of creatures, she's the daintiest of misses,
With her pretty patent leathers or her alligator ties,
With her eyes inviting glances and her lips inviting kisses,
As she wanders by the ocean or strolls under country skies.

She's a captivating dresser, and her parasols are stunning,
Her fads will take your breath away, her hats are dreams of style;
She is not so very bookish, but with repartee and punning
She can set the savants laughing and make even dudelets smile.

She has no attacks of talent, she is not a stage-struck maiden;
She is wholly free from hobbies, and she dreams of no "career;"

She is mostly gay and happy, never sad or care-
beladen,
Though she sometimes sighs a little if a gentle-
man is near.

She's a sturdy little walker and she braves all
kinds of weather,
And when the rain or fog or mist drive rival
crimps a-wreck,
Her fluffy hair goes curling like a kinked-up ostrich
feather
Around her ears and forehead and the white
nape of her neck.

She is like a fish in water; she can handle reins
and racket;
From head to toe and finger-tips she's thoroughly
alive;
When she goes promenading in a most distracting
jacket,
The rustle round her feet suggests how laun-
dresses may thrive.

She can dare the wind and sunshine in the most
bravado manner,
And after hours of sailing she has merely cheeks
of rose;
Old Sol himself seems smitten and at most will
only tan her,
Though to everybody else he gives a danger-
signal nose.

She's a trifle sentimental, and she's fond of admiration,
And she sometimes flirts a little in the season's giddy whirl ;
But win her if you can, sir, she may prove your life's salvation,
For an angel masquerading oft is she, the summer girl.

"THE BEAUTIFUL BLUE DANUBE."

[With "Blue Danube Waltz" as musical accompaniment.]

THEY drift down the hall together,
He smiles in her lifted eyes;
Like waves of that mighty river,
The strains of the "Danube" rise.
They float on its rhythmic measure,
Like leaves on a summer stream;
And here, in this scene of pleasure,
I bury my sweet, dead dream.

Through the cloud of her dusky tresses,
Like a star shines out her face;
And the form his strong arm presses,
Is sylph-like in its grace.
As a leaf on the bounding river
Is lost on the seething sea,
I know that forever and ever
My dream is lost to me.

And still the viols are playing
That grand old wordless rhyme;
And still those two are swaying
In perfect tune and time.

If the great bassoons that mutter,
  If the clarionets that blow,
Were given a voice to utter
  The secret things they know,

Would the lists of the slain who slumber
  On the Danube's battle-plains
The unknown hosts outnumber
  Who die, 'neath the "Danube's" strains?
Those fall where cannons rattle,
  'Mid the rain of shot and shell;
But these, in a fiercer battle,
  Find death in the music's swell.

With the river's roar of passion
  Is blended the dying groan;
But here, in the halls of fashion,
  Hearts break and make no moan.
And the music, swelling and sweeping,
  Like the river, knows it all;
But none are counting or keeping
  The lists of those who fall

THE BIRTH OF THE OPAL.

THE Sunbeam loved the Moonbeam,
And followed her low and high;
But the Moonbeam fled and hid her head—
She was so shy, so shy.

The Sunbeam wooed with passion,
Ah! he was a lover bold;
And his heart was afire with mad desire
For the Moonbeam, pale and cold.

She fled like a dream before him,
Her hair was a shining sheen;
And, oh, that Fate would annihilate
The space that lay between!

Just as the Day lay panting
In the arms of the Twilight dim,
The Sunbeam caught the one he sought
And drew her close to him.

But out of his warm arms startled,
And stirred by love's first shock,
She sprang afraid, like a trembling maid,
And hid in the niche of a rock.

And the Sunbeam followed and found her,
  And led her to love's own feast,
And they were wed on that rocky bed,
  And the dying Day was their priest.

And, lo! the beautiful Opal,
  That rare and wondrous gem,
Where the Moon and Sun blend into one,
  Is the child that was born to them.

SOUNDS FROM THE BASEBALL FIELD.

BATTER in the home place,
That was nobly done;
Try and get the first base—
Run! Run! RUN!
Ah, there, short stop, will you miss?
Hear the people cheer and hiss,
Hear them yell and shout.
Twinkling legs and flying feet—
(Oh, I wonder who will beat!)
Faster, faster, out!
Umpire, umpire, go along;
That was wrong, sir, that was wrong.

Pitcher pitches, four balls,
"Take your base, my man."
Toward the second now he crawls—
"Steal it if you can."
Oh, the ball has gone so high,
Can they catch it on the fly?
Ah, there is no doubt,
He will get his third, I vow—
Pshaw! the ball has got there now,
"Two men out!"
Umpire, umpire, that was wrong;
Go along, sir, go along.

One man on the first base,
  Not a single run.
Boys are warming to the race—
  Now look out for fun.
Pitcher's arm maybe is tired;
Batter sudden seems inspired,
  Grounds the ball to win.
Run there, run there, run your best,
I am screaming with the rest:
  "Two men in!"
Umpire, umpire, go away;
Dead wrong, dead wrong, sir, I say.

What's the matter now, pray?
  Taking breath, that's all;
But the restless people say
  "Play ball, play ball."
One ball, two strikes, two balls—"Foul'
Umpire calls, and people howl:
  "What is he about?"
Run, run, run, run, Run, Run, RUN!
Half the inning now is done,
  "Three men out!"
Umpire, umpire, go along;
You are always, always wrong.

A WALTZ-QUADRILLE.

[With Musical Accompaniment.]

THE band was playing a waltz-quadrille ;
I felt as light us a wind-blown feather,
As we floated away at the caller's will,
Through the intricate, mazy dance together.
Like mimic armies our lines were meeting,
Slowly advancing, and then retreating
All decked in their bright array ;
And back and forth to the music's rhyme
We moved together, and all the time
I knew you were going away.

The fold of your strong arm sent a thrill
From heart to brain as we gently glided,
Like leaves, on the wave of that waltz-quadrille,
Parted, met, and again divided—
You drifting one way, and I another :
Then suddenly turning and facing each other ;
Then off in the blithe chassée;
Then airily back to our places swaying,
While every beat of the music seemed saying
That you were going away.

I said to my heart : " Let us take our fill
  Of mirth, and music, and love and laughter;
For it all must end with this waltz-quadrille,
  And life will be never the same life after.
    Oh, that the caller might go on calling,
    Oh, that the music might go on falling
      Like a shower of silver spray,
    While we whirled on to the vast Forever,
    Where no heart breaks, and no ties sever,
      And no one goes away."

A clamor, a crash, and the band was still—
  'Twas the end of the dream, and the end of the measure;
The last low notes of that waltz-quadrille
  Seemed like a dirge o'er the death of Pleasure.
    You said good-night, and the spell was over—
    Too warm for a friend, and too cold for a lover—
      There was nothing else to say;
    But the lights looked dim, and the dancers weary,
    And the music was sad and, the hall was dreary,
      After you went away.

ANSWERED.

GOOD-BYE—yes, I am going.
Sudden? Well, you are right;
But a startling truth came home to me
With sudden force last night.
What is it? Shall I tell you—
Nay, that is why I go;
I am running away from the battle-field,
Turning my back on the foe.

Riddles? You think me cruel!
Have you not been most kind?
Why, when you question me like that
What answer can I find?
You fear you failed to amuse me,
Your husband's friend and guest,
Whom he bade you entertain and please?
Well, you have done your best.

Then why am I going? Listen:
A friend of mine abroad,
Whose theories I have been acting upon,
Has proven himself a fraud.

You have heard me quote from Plato
  A thousand times, no doubt ;
Well, I have discovered he did not know
  What he was talking about.

You think I am speaking strangely ?
  You cannot understand ?
Well, let me look down into your eyes,
  And let me hold your hand.
I am running away from danger—
  I am flying before I fall ;
I am going because with heart and soul
  I love you—that is all.
There, now, you are white with anger ;
  I knew it would be so.
You should not question a man too close
  When he tells you he must go.

THE SIGN-BOARD.

I WILL paint you a sign, rumseller,
And hang it above your door ;
A truer and better signboard
Than ever you had before.
I will paint with the skill of a master,
And many shall pause to see
This wonderful piece of painting,
So like the reality.

I will paint yourself, rumseller,
As you wait for that fair young boy,
Just in the morning of manhood,
A mother's pride and joy.
He has no thought of stopping,
But you greet him with a smile,
And you seem so blithe and friendly,
That he pauses to chat awhile.

I will paint you again, rumseller,
I will paint you as you stand,
With a foaming glass of liquor
Extended in your hand.

He wavers, but you urge him—
  Drink, pledge me just this one!
And he takes the glass and drains it,
  And the hellish work is done.

And next I will paint a drunkard—
  Only a year has flown,
But into that loathsome creature
  The fair young boy has grown.
The work was sure and rapid.
  I will paint him as he lies
In a torpid, drunken slumber,
  Under the wintry skies.

I will paint the form of the mother
  As she kneels at her darling's side,
Her beautiful boy that was dearer
  Than all the world beside.
I will paint the shape of a coffin,
  Labeled with one word—" lost,"
I will paint all this, rumseller,
  And will paint it free of cost.

The sin and the shame and the sorrow,
  The crime and the want and the woe
That are born there in your workshop,
  No hand can paint, you know.
But I'll paint you a sign, rumseller,
  And many shall pause to view
This wonderful swinging signboard,
  So terribly, fearfully true.

ABOUT MAY.

ONE night Nurse Sleep held out her hand
To tired little May.
"Come, go with me to Wonderland,"
She said, "I know the way.
Just rock-a-by—hum—m—m,
And lo! we come
To the place where the dream-girls play."

But naughty May, she wriggled away
From Sleep's soft arms, and said:
"I must stay awake till I eat my cake,
And then I will go to bed;
With a by-lo, away I will go."
But the good nurse shook her head.

She shook her head and away she sped,
While May sat munching her crumb.
But after the cake there came an ache,
Though May cried: "Come, Sleep, come,
And it's oh! my! let us by-lo-by"—
All save the echoes were dumb.

She ran after Sleep toward Wonderland,
Ran till the morning light;
And just as she caught her and grasped her hand,
A nightmare gave her a fright.
And it's by-lo, I hope she'll know
Better another night.

THE GIDDY GIRL.

[This recitation is intended to be given with an accompaniment of waltz music, introducing dance-steps at the refrain: "With one, two, three," etc.]

A GIDDY young maiden with nimble feet,
Heigh-ho! alack and alas!
Declared she would far rather dance than eat,
And the truth of it came to pass.
For she danced all day and she danced all night;
She danced till the green earth faded white;
She danced ten partners out of breath;
She danced the eleventh one quite to death;
And still she redowaed up and down—
The giddiest girl in town.
With one, two, three; one, two, three; one, two, three—kick;
Chassée back, chassée back, whirl around quick.

The name of this damsel ended with E—
Heigh-ho! alack and a-day!
And she was as fair as a maiden need be,
Till she danced her beauty away.

She danced her big toes out of joint ;
She danced her other toes all to a point ;
She danced out slipper and boot and shoe ;
She danced till the bones of her feet came through.
And still she redowaed, waltzed and whirled—
The giddiest girl in the world.
With one, two, three ; one, two, three ; one, two,
three—kick ;
Chassée back, chassée back, whirl around quick.

Now the end of my story is sad to relate—
Heigh-ho ! and away we go !
For this beautiful maiden's final fate
Is shrouded in gloom and woe.
She danced herself into a patent top ;
She whirled and whirled till she could not stop ;
She danced and bounded and sprang so far,
That she stuck at last on a pointed star ;
And there she must dance till the Judgment Day,
And after it, too, for she danced away
Her soul, you see, so she has no place anywhere
out of space,
With her one, two, three ; one, two, three ; one, two,
three—kick ;
Chassée back, chassée back, whirl about quick.

DELL AND I.

IN a mansion grand, just over the way,
Lives bonny, beautiful Dell;
You may have heard of this lady gay,
For she is a famous belle.
I live in a low cot opposite,
You never have heard of me;
For when the lady moon shines bright,
Who would a pale star see?
But ah, well, ah, well! I am happier far than Dell,
As strange as that may be.

Dell has robes of the richest kind—
Pinks and purples and blues.
And she worries her maid and frets her mind
To know which one to choose.
Which shall it be now, silk or lace?
In which will I be most fair?
She stands by the mirror with anxious face,
And her maid looks on in despair.
Ah, well, ah, well! I am not worried, you see, like Dell,
For I have but *one* to wear.

Dell has lovers of every grade,
  Of every age and style ;
Suitors flutter about the maid,
  And bask in her word and smile.
She keeps them all, with a coquette's art,
  As suits her mood or mirth,
And vainly wonders if in *one* heart
  Of all true love has birth.
Ah, well, ah, well! I never question myself like Dell,
  For I *know* a true heart's worth.

Pleasure to Dell seems stale and old,
  Often she sits and sighs ;
Life to me is a tale untold,
  Each day is a glad surprise.
Dell will marry, of course, some day
  After her belleship is run ;
She will cavil the matter in worldly way
  And wed Dame Fortune's son.
But, ah, well, sweet to tell, I shall not dally and choose like Dell,
  For I love and am loved by—*one.*

VANITY FAIR.

IN Vanity Fair, as we bow and smile,
As we talk of the opera after the weather,
As we chat of fashion and fad and style,
We know we are playing a part together.
You know that the mirth she wears, she borrows;
She knows you laugh but to hide your sorrows;
We know that under the silks and laces,
And back of beautiful, beaming faces,
Lie secret trouble and grim despair,
In Vanity Fair.

In Vanity Fair, on dress parade,
Our colors look bright and our swords are gleaming;
But many a uniform's worn and frayed,
And most of the weapons, despite their seeming,
Are dull and blunted and badly battered,
And close inspection will show how tattered
And stained are the banners that float above us.
Our comrades hate, while they swear to love us;
And robed like Pleasure walks gaunt-eyed Care,
In Vanity Fair.

In Vanity Fair, as we strive for place,
  As we rush and jostle and crowd and hurry,
We know the goal is not worth the race—
  We know the prize is not worth the worry;
That all our gain means loss for another;
That in fighting for self we wound each other;
That the crown of success weighs hard and presses
The brow of the victor with thorns—not caresses;
That honors are empty and worthless to wear,
                    In Vanity Fair.

But in Vanity Fair, as we pass along,
  We meet strong hearts that are worth the knowing;
'Mong poor paste jewels that deck the throng,
  We see a solitaire sometimes glowing.
We find grand souls under robes of fashion,
'Neath light demeanors hide strength and passion;
And fair fine honor and Godlike resistance,
In halls of pleasure may have existence;
And we find pure altars and shrines of prayer,
                    In Vanity Fair.

A GIRL'S AUTUMN REVERIE.

WE plucked a red rose, you and I,
All in the summer weather.
Sweet its perfume and rare its bloom,
Enjoyed by us together.
The rose is dead, the summer fled,
And bleak winds are complaining;
We dwell apart, but in each heart
We find the thorn remaining.

We sipped a sweet wine, you and I,
All in the summer weather.
The beaded draught we lightly quaffed,
And filled the glass together.
Together watched its rosy glow,
And saw its bubbles glitter;
Apart, alone, we only know
The lees are very bitter.

We walked in sunshine, you and I,
All in the summer weather.
The very night seemed noonday bright
When we two were together.

I wonder why with our good-by
  O'er hill and vale and meadow
There fell such shade, our paths seemed laid
  Forevermore in shadow.

We dreamed a sweet dream, you and I,
  All in the summer weather,
Where rose and wine and warm sunshine
  Were mingled in together.
We dreamed that June was with us yet,
  We woke to find December.
We dreamed that we two could forget,
  We woke but to remember.

GETHSEMANE.

IN golden youth, when seems the earth
A summer land of singing mirth,
When souls are glad and hearts are light,
And not a shadow lurks in sight,
We do not know it, but there lies,
Somewhere veiled under evening skies,
A garden all must sometime see—
The garden of Gethsemane.

With joyous steps we go our ways;
Love lends a halo to our days.
Light sorrows sail like clouds afar,
We laugh and say how strong we are!
We hurry on, and, hurrying, go
Close to the borderland of woe
That waits for you, and waits for me,
Forever waits—Gethsemane.

Down shadowy lanes, across strange streams,
Bridged over by our broken dreams,
Behind the misty caps of years,
Beyond the great salt fount of tears

The garden lies. Strive as you may,
You cannot miss it in your way.
All paths that have been or may be,
Pass somewhere through Gethsemane.

All those who journey, soon or late,
Must pass within the garden's gate;
Must kneel alone in darkness there,
And battle with some fierce despair.
God pity those who cannot say
"Not mine but Thine;" who only pray
"Let this cup pass," and cannot see
The *purpose* in Gethsemane.

THE COMING MAN.

OH, not for the great departed,
  Who formed our country's laws,
And not for the bravest-hearted
  Who died in freedom's cause,
And not for some living hero
  To whom all bend the knee,
My muse would raise her song of praise—
  But for the man *to be.*

For out of the strife which woman
  Is passing through to-day,
A man that is more than human
  Shall yet be born, I say.
A man in whose pure spirit
  No dross of self will lurk;
A man who is strong to cope with wrong,
  A man who is proud to work.

A man with hope undaunted,
  A man with godlike power,
Shall come when he most is wanted,
  Shall come at the needed hour.

He shall silence the din and clamor
  Of clan disputing with clan,
And toil's long fight with purse-proud might
  Shall triumph through this man.

I know he is coming, coming,
  To help, to guide, to save.
Though I hear no martial drumming,
  And see no flags that wave.
But the great soul travail of woman,
  And the bold free thought unfurled,
Are heralds that say he is on the way—
  The coming man of the world.

Mourn not for vanished ages
  With their great heroic men,
Who dwell in history's pages
  And live in the poet's pen.
For the grandest times are before us,
  And the world is yet to see
The noblest worth of this old earth
  In the men that are to be.

A MAN'S REPENTANCE.

[Intended for recitation at club dinners.]

TO-NIGHT when I came from the club at
eleven,
Under the gaslight I saw a face—
A woman's face! and I swear to heaven
It looked like the ghastly ghost of—
Grace!

And Grace? why, Grace was fair; and I tarried,
And loved her a season as we men do.
And then—but pshaw! why, of course, she is
married,
Has a husband and doubtless a babe or two.

She was perfectly calm on the day we parted;
She spared me a scene, to my great surprise.
She wasn't the kind to be broken-hearted,
I remember she said, with a spark in her eyes.

I was tempted, I know, by her proud defiance
To make good my promises there and then.
But the world would have called it a mésalliance!
I dreaded the comments and sneers of men.

So I left her to grieve for a faithless lover,
And to hide her heart from the cold world's
sight

As women do hide them, the wide earth over.
  My God! *was* it Grace that I saw to-night?

I thought of her married, and often, with pity,
  A poor man's wife in some dull place.
And now to know she is here in the city,
  Under the gaslight, and with *that* face!

Yet I knew it at once, in spite of the daubing
  Of paint and powder, and she knew me;
She drew a quick breath that was almost sobbing,
  And shrank in the shade so I should not see.

There was hell in her eyes! She was worn and jaded;
  Her soul is at war with the life she has led.
As I looked on that face so strangely faded,
  I wonder God did not strike me dead.

While I have been happy and gay and jolly,
  Received by the very best people in town,
That girl whom I led in the way to folly
  Has gone on recklessly down and down.

Two o'clock, and no sleep has found me.
  That face I saw in the street-lamp's light
Peers everywhere out from the shadows around me—
  I know how a murderer feels to-night!

DICK'S FAMILY.

WHEN Dick, the little deformed invalid, hobbled from his bed into his chair-lounge at the window, where he reclined all day long, he saw a rosy-cheeked young woman polishing the windows across the street.

His pale face tinged with a sudden glow, and his painfully brilliant eyes shone with an increased lustre.

"Well, I *declare* if my house isn't occupied!" he cried, and he lifted the window and peered across the way with such an excited countenance, that the young woman opposite paused in her work to regard him. But after a moment's observation the startled look in her face gave place to pity, for she saw that the great shining eyes were those of an invalid—an invalid child, she thought.

"Poor child; poor little fellow," she said to herself, "and such a pretty face, too!"

But Dick was twenty-two years old, with a man's

heart and a man's longings shut up in his deformed body. But since he was compelled to pass his days between a bed and a chair, with an occasional hour down on the curbing in the sunlight of a warm day, he found his whole enjoyment in his imagination. And wonderful flights it took, flights and freaks suspected by no one save good old Dr. Griffin, his one confidant.

He had known Dick ever since his advent into his life of misery. Dick's mother had been the beauty of the street more than a score of years ago. Old Benjamin Levy, her father, was a hard man, and to escape the barren home and dreary life, pretty Josie eloped with a handsome Christian whom she had met while promenading on the street. Her father had uttered a terrible curse when the knowledge of her flight came to him; and scarce two years later the curse had fallen, for pretty Josie came home to die, and to leave her invalid baby as the constant reminder of the fulfilment of his curse, to her father.

Dr. Griffin had been retained during all these years as Dick's physician; for the one thing in which old Benjamin showed no parsimony was in the care of this little deformed grandchild. A little shop where he sold second-hand clothing, and a couple of small rooms above it, for living purposes constituted his *ménage.*

Directly opposite was a three-story and basement brick house, which had in its day been a semi-fashionable private residence. But as trade encroached upon the street, this building had degenerated to an apartment house.

While the house stood tenantless' Dick amused himself by imagining that it was his own residence.

"It is my house," he would say, "and I am traveling abroad, and it is closed. By and by I shall come home, and there will be a great house-warmin', and lights in every window and flower-pots on the sills, and pretty curtains and life and fun; for I am a very rich young man with lots of money, and I always have everything very gay around me."

Dr. Griffin used to encourage the boy in his fancies, thinking they relieved the monotony of his dreary life. "Well, I see you are still traveling abroad, Dick," he used to say. "That house of yours is still closed. No idea when you will return, have you?"

"No, I'm havin' too good a time to come back yet awhile," Dick would answer. "Haven't half seen the world yet."

But one day there were people moving about on the ground floor of the house, and Dick heard his grandfather say it was to be made into flats, and let to separate families.

The next time Dr. Griffin called, he greeted the boy with—

"Hello! Dick, welcome home! I see you have returned from abroad."

Dick shook his head soberly. "Oh, no!" he replied, "I am not back yet. But I got tired of havin' my house stay empty—thought I might as well let it help pay my expenses (it's awful expensive travelin', you know), so I've got some tenants in the house. Goin' to let each floor separate, 'cause it is too expensive a house for anybody to take whole, 'cept some rich feller like me."

During the last six months the floor exactly opposite Dick's window had been vacant. After three months had passed without a tenant, he told Dr. Griffin that he had decided to reserve that floor for his own use.

"I'm goin' to come home pretty soon and settle down, you see," he said, "and so I thought I'd keep that floor for myself. I don't need the whole house, and I can just as well let the other tenants stay."

And now, after three months more had passed, here were people moving into his apartments!

Dr. Griffin called that very afternoon, and found Dick looking unusually animated.

"Well, well, Dick!" he exclaimed. "So, after all you've decided to rent your apartments? You have neighbors, I see. I fear you will never return now and settle down as you intended."

"Why, that's no neighbors, Doctor," replied Dick, contemptuously; "that's my family. I've come home to stay, and brought my family, you see."

"You don't tell me so! Why, what a stupid old fellow I am, to be sure!" cried the Doctor, with feigned self-scorn. "How large a family have you, Dick?"

"Well, only—only one, as I care 'specially about. Look—look at her, Doctor!" catching the Doctor s hand and leaning forward in his chair. "See her a-fixin' the nice little curtain at the window? She's a regular neat one, she is, my little woman over there. She was a-cleanin' the windows and things this mornin' with her hair so slick and a span clean apron on. That's the kind of girl I like. I allers liked that kind. Isn't she the right kind, eh, Doctor?"

Dr. Griffin saw a trim young woman with rosy cheeks, looping back scrim curtains with pink ribbons. He nodded gravely.

"From my brief acquaintance, I should say she was," he answered. "I congratulate you on your good luck. With such a family as that, you ought to be a happy fellow!"

"Queer little fellow; queer little fellow," he said to himself, as he went down the stairs. "Strange notion that about his home and family."

When Dick awoke the following day he felt a new sense of happiness in the thought of his neighbor opposite. He hurried through his tedious ceremony of dressing, ate his frugal breakfast, hobbled into his invalid-chair, and gave an eager glance across the street. Yes, there were the dainty curtains still at the window, so it was no dream. He watched for a glimpse of the occupant, but she did not appear. Then he laughed a little softly to himself.

"Of course, she wouldn't be hangin' around the window at all hours; she isn't that sort; and, of course, I'm over there now, and she's a-pourin' coffee for me; we take breakfast sort of late to-day, 'cause we're just home from Europe, and I haven't gone down to the office yet. After I get off she'll brush around and set things to right, and —hello! I must have gone now you know for there she is a-whiskin' the dust off the window-sill as pretty as ever and as neat as a pin. All the time I'm down at the office with them pesky clerks of mine a-botherin' me I'll be thinkin' of that sweet little woman up here waitin' for me."

"We do have very sociable times," Dick told the Doctor a month later. "That little woman and I seem made for each other. She's just the right sort. We never have no fusses, and things go so comfortable-like all the time."

"And how do you like the other party? There's a man there also, I see. How do you like him?"

Dick flushed painfully, and a deep frown settled on his face. There was a man whom he saw from time to time sitting at the window after the dinner hour reading his paper. But the moment he made his appearance, Dick closed his eyes or left the window seat. He regarded the man as an intruder

—a shadow upon his home life, a serpent in his Eden.

Sunday was a day of restlessness and discontent, because the man was there all day long, and on Sundays he avoided the invalid-chair, which was his seat on all other days. Now, when he heard Dr. Griffin speak of the man as a real being, he suffered all the bitter and mortifying pangs of jealousy which might come to a man who hears a stranger give words to a suspicion of his wife's disloyalty to which he has striven to blind himself.

"A man—a—yes—there's a man there sometimes," Dick stammered; "he's a—a sort of poor relative, don't you know. One of my relations, you see, and I can't very well turn him off."

"Oh, I see," answered the Doctor, noticing Dick's confusion and hastening to help him out. "Well, everybody has some one of that sort. I've half a dozen poor relatives who live on me Some one of them is with us most of the time. A little uncomfortable occasionally may be, because every man's house is his castle where he wants to be alone at times. But we who have homes have no right to be selfish; we must share them with less fortunate people. Happiness must not make us selfish."

Dick's face brightened. His heart had grown light and happy while the Doctor spoke.

"That's just what I tell myself and the little woman," he said. "Often she doesn't like to have the fellow droppin' in and spoilin' our chats" (Dick felt an immense satisfaction in saying this), "but I tell her with just our two selves we'd get selfish with happiness unless we had somethin' to do for another. But he does break up our Sundays awfully—scarcely can get a word alone, that fellow's pokin' around so."

"Oh, well, you can afford him one day in the week, and I wouldn't let him bother me ; just be as happy as if he wasn't around."

Somehow Dick felt much better after this talk. He had tried to ignore the presence of the man opposite, but now he could acknowledge it, and definitely locate the man in his thought as a poor dependent, who was benefitted by his bounty. He enjoyed thinking that the little woman objected more or less to the fellow, and that she allowed him so much liberty only to please Dick. As the weeks rolled on he confessed to the Doctor that the fellow was really useful at times.

"Rainy days he goes to market for the little woman," he said, "and often runs out on errands for us."

"Dick's house" had been occupied six months when a whole week passed without his seeing his "little woman" at the window. During that six months there had scarcely been an afternoon during which she had not sat for an hour or two at the window with her sewing. Dick had grown to think of that hour as the bright spoke in the wheel of the day. She looked at him so kindly and gently, and he used to imagine he was lying on a lounge in the room, reading aloud to her as she sewed, and that her kind, warm smile was one of love, not of pity. And when a whole week passed without his once seeing her, Dick found himself in a nervous fever, with a blinding headache from having gazed so eagerly and anxiously across the street, and Grandfather Levy sent for Dr. Griffin.

"There's somethin' the matter over the way," whispered Dick, as soon as the Doctor was alone with him. "I haven't seen her for a whole week; there's a strange woman there, and I'm sure she's sick. I couldn't sleep all last night for worryin' about her."

Dr. Griffin went to the window and looked out. Then he took a magnifying glass from his pocket, and deliberately stared into the window opposite.

Then he went back to Dick. "My dear fellow," he said, "you are to be congratulated. You are a father. I saw the nurse walking up and down the room with the child in her arms. It is a bad habit, by the way, and you must tell her not to teach it to the child. You can't begin too young with them."

After the Doctor went away, Dick buried his face in his pillow and wept softly.

"A little baby—yes, my little baby," he whispered. "God bless the little woman. Some day she will sit with it at the window, and I shall have them both for company."

And then one day, a soft, warm day, late in May, there she sat at the window again, with lilies instead of roses in her cheeks, and the bundle of flannel in her arms. She smiled at Dick, and tears of joy and love welled up in his eyes as he gazed upon the two.

"I've got two of 'em for company now, the little woman and the baby," he whispered.

After that the days seemed very happy and bright, and Dick thought himself the richest man on earth. Only he wondered why the roses did not come back to the little woman's cheeks.

"She doesn't look as well as she ought to," he told the Doctor one day in June, and the Doctor, peering over his spectacles, shook his head as he looked at her, but Dick did not see it.

Passing down the block one day, Dr. Griffin came face to face with a little girl who wheeled a baby carriage, and, as he glanced under the awning, he was startled to see two weirdly brilliant eyes, the very counterpart of Dick's, gazing up at him.

"Whose child is this? Does it live over in the brick flats there?" queried the Doctor.

The little girl nodded.

"Second flight up?"

"Yes, sir."

"Queer enough, queer enough," he mused, as he walked on.

"Your baby has eyes exactly like you, Dick," said the Doctor, a few days later. "Honestly, no joking; I saw the little fellow on the street and knew him by his eyes."

After that Dick's heart went out to the baby more and more, and he was eager to see it. One day he saw the little nurse-girl wheeling the carriage, and as fast as his lame body would permit he hurried and hobbled down to the street, hoping it would pass near him. Sure enough it did, and Dick's heart jumped into his throat as he leaned on his cane and peered into the carriage to catch his first glimpse of the baby he had grown to think of as his own. Yes, those were his own eyes—his very own gazing up at him, and he touched the little hand with reverence and awe. The baby laughed and twisted its small soft fingers about his thumb, and clung to his hand as if unwilling to let him go. For weeks after that he would wake at night, thinking he felt that clinging touch upon his hand; and those great dark, startled eyes, the very counterpart of his own, seemed illuminating the night for him.

It was early November when he failed to see the baby at the window or on the street; nor did the mother appear at the window for four days. The morning of the fifth day, Dick saw from his window a little white hearse drawn by white ponies pause at the house opposite, and then some one came out with a small casket followed

by the "male relative" and a few sad-faced friends.

That day Dick entered Gethsemane, and the mourners who followed the little baby to its last resting-place shed no bitterer tears than he. Mixed with his keen anguish for the loss of the child was fear for the life of the mother who was too ill to attend the burial.

That night Dr. Griffin was sent for, and he found Dick so ill and feverish that he was alarmed. His tears mingled with Dick's, when the poor boy told him of the baby's death, and begged him to go over and inquire after the "little woman."

"You can ask the janitor, Doctor; just say friends opposite want to inquire after her; you needn't say no more."

The Doctor did as Dick desired, and came back shortly, making an effort to speak cheerfully.

"The janitor says Mrs.—"

"The little woman," interrupted Dick. "Yes, yes; how is she?" Not for worlds would he have heard her name spoken.

"She is ill, suffering from a prostration caused by grief," the Doctor replied. "But she is young, and she will rally in a few weeks no doubt. You must brace up, old man, and be ready to comfort her. If you don't look after yourself a little better I won't promise for the consequences to your health. You've overtaxed yourself lately, and you must keep very quiet now for a few days."

But each day Dick dragged himself to the window to see if the little woman was visible. And on the tenth day after the baby's funeral, a black hearse with nodding black plumes, and black horses with jet harness and dangling black tassels, stood at the house opposite; and Dick, with panting breath and wild eyes, crawled down the stairs, and out upon the street, for he seemed choking in the house, and he thought he must hinder those cruel people from taking away the little woman. He could not, could not let her go from him forever, and when he saw them lifting the casket into the hearse, he reached out his arms, tried to cry out and stop them, and then he fell over weak and helpless, with strange sounds ringing in his ears and warm blood spurting from his mouth. When he awoke to consciousness he was lying on his couch, and Dr. Griffin and Grandfather Levy were bending over him with tears in their eyes.

He tried to speak, and with each syllable the blood gushed again from his lips.

"You mustn't talk," said the Doctor. "You are very weak and it may be fatal to you if you do not keep quiet."

He drew the Doctor's head down close to his lips.

"It's no use tryin' to save me," he whispered. "I'd rather go—I couldn't stand it livin' on with both of 'em gone. I've nothin' to live for now—no ambition or pleasure left. I've had all the pleasure

I'll ever get out of life, Doctor, this year back. It's kinder to let me go—and—follow my family."

The hemorrhage set in anew, and with the red gushing tide, Dick's soul passed out to seek those of the little woman and the baby.

www.ingramcontent.com/pod-product-compliance
Lightning Source LLC
LaVergne TN
LVHW021403110826
845150LV00007B/1762

* 9 7 8 1 4 2 5 5 1 2 3 4 7 *